Felbrigg Hall

Norfolk

John Maddison

☘ THE NATIONAL TRUST

Contrasts and characters

'I have never stayed in any other house where there was such an atmosphere of peace and serenity.'

Brinsley Ford, who visited Felbrigg in the 1950s

It is not possible to look at the Jacobean south front of Felbrigg for more than a few minutes without being struck by the extraordinary disparity of its fabric. The Norfolk weather has torn and scratched at its ancient surface, revealing not only the successive decorations of past owners but good and bad repairs, and great sections of wall made up of widely differing materials: brick, plaster, pebbles, flints, rusting iron and wonderfully wrought limestone. Here is human geology; an appealing mixture of man and nature in which the natural elements seem gradually to be getting the upper hand.

The Jacobean mason with his pattern-book classicism and his deep attachment to the mullioned oriels of the Gothic past touches us with his sincerity. But if we walk round to the south-west corner, we are suddenly confronted by the immaculate brick façade of the 1680s 'New Appartment' standing like an entirely different house. A cultivated and cosmopolitan product of the Restoration, it ostentatiously ignores its slightly dishevelled elderly relative and stares resolutely across the ha-ha. This is a house of surprising contrasts and strong characters.

A picturesque patchwork. The early 17th-century south front

Key dates and people

1621–4: The south front is built for *Thomas Windham* out of the carcass of an early Tudor building.

1680s: Thomas's son, *William Windham I*, dramatically extends the Jacobean house with the new red-brick west wing, employing the virtuoso William Samwell as his architect and decorating its interiors with wonderful plaster-work, but neither architect nor patron lives to see its completion.

Early 18th century: William I's son, *Ashe Windham,* who had succeeded in 1689, builds the Orangery and the new service courtyard on the east side of the house. He also completes the interior of the west wing.

1749–61: William Windham II had returned from an extensive and eventful Grand Tour in 1742, weighed down with books and pictures. On his father Ashe's death in 1749, William engages the architect James Paine to refashion

the interiors to accommodate his new possessions, and to put up a new east service wing. Paine's Rococo rooms are amongst the most satisfying of their period, and were little altered after William's early death in 1761.

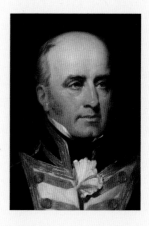

Early 19th century: William II's son, William Windham III, becomes a leading politician, but does little to Felbrigg. He dies in 1810, leaving the estate to his nephew, *Vice-Admiral William Lukin,* on condition that he change his name to Windham. In 1824 the Admiral employs W. J. Donthorn to remodel Paine's service wing with Gothic windows and to build a new neo-Tudor stable block. In the 1840s his son William Howe Windham alters the Great Hall – the last significant architectural change at Felbrigg.

1854–1923: In spite of Felbrigg's rapid decline during the period of the eccentric spendthrift 'Mad Windham', who inherited in 1854, its sale to John Ketton in 1863, and a period of unchecked decay at the beginning of the 20th century, the house and its contents survive substantially intact.

1923–69: The Ketton-Cremer family, to whom the estate passed in 1923, sets about the gradual repair of a very rundown establishment in spite of limited means. The last scholar-squire of Felbrigg, *Robert Wyndham Ketton-Cremer,* carries on this work, devoting himself to the place. When he dies in 1969, he leaves the estate, the house and its contents to the National Trust.

Tour of the House

The Exterior

The South Front

This, the earliest part of the house, was begun in about 1620 and incorporates remains of the previous Tudor house. It is built of a mixture of brick, flint and pebble with dressings in a fine oolitic Ketton limestone from Northamptonshire. The arms above the entrance are those of Sir John Wyndham (1558–1645), of Orchard Wyndham in Somerset, impaling those of Joan Portman, his wife, and of their son Thomas Windham (1585–1654) and his first wife Elizabeth Lytton, whom he married in 1620.

The design has much in common with the architecture of Blickling Hall, which was being built simultaneously, and many of the details are identical, as were some of the craftsmen. The Great Hall lies to the left of the porch, and behind the bay window to the right originally

(Below) The south front (on the right) contrasts with the red-brick west front of the 1680s (on the left). Beyond to the right lies the stable block

lay the kitchen and pantry. Above the Great Hall on the first floor was probably the Great Chamber (replaced in the 1750s by the Library). The upper part of the front was being completed in 1624, when the stone lions on the gables were provided. The inscription 'Gloria Deo in Excelsis' may relate to the re-establishment of the Windhams at Felbrigg by Sir John Wyndham of Orchard after a period of decline and misfortune in which the Norfolk branch died out.

The front was rendered by W. J. Donthorn for Admiral Windham in about 1825 and beneath this protective coating, which is gradually deteriorating, are substantial traces of earlier treatments.

The East Front

This reveals the substantial extension to the rear of the Jacobean house built by William Windham I in 1675. It copied the side gables of the Jacobean front but was entirely of brick. The east bay was altered by William Windham III in 1809, when William Collins made alterations to the rooms on this side.

The East Wing

This service wing was built by Paine for William Windham II in 1749 and replaced a narrower range, which his father Ashe had built by about 1710. Paine's design was Palladian in character: a pedimented centre and semicircular 'therm' windows, with an open arcade in front. In 1825 Donthorn remodelled the arcade, built the pavilions and enclosed the open walk with Gothic windows to make a corridor.

The Stable Block

Built in 1824–5 for Admiral Windham by Donthorn. The neo-Tudor scheme was originally rendered, but nearly all of this render has fallen off since about 1900. The screen closes a courtyard which had carriage-houses in the centre flanked by wings containing stalls and loose boxes. The right-hand wing was converted many years ago into a house, and the left-hand one, deprived long-since of its stable fittings, was used by the gardeners. In 1989 the carriage-houses were converted into a restaurant by the National Trust, and in 1993 the two wings became an additional cafeteria and the shop. The stalls in the north-west corner have been restored, and the loose box in which R. W. Ketton-Cremer's brother Dick kept his horse, Jester, has been preserved.

The West Front

Designs for the extension of the Jacobean house were presented to William Windham I in 1674 by the gentleman architect William Samwell. Samwell died in 1676 and this new front was probably not built until the mid-1680s. The right-hand lead rainwater head is dated 1686. The extension absorbed the rear portion of the Jacobean house. Its beautifully proportioned classicism and superb brickwork make an arresting contrast with the old front, but the difference may have been less at first, if the earlier

(Right) The Orangery

work retained its red colourwash. Samwell's elevation drawing shows a figure of Hercules standing in a niche between the two central first-floor windows, and the texture of the brickwork here suggests that such a feature may once have existed. On the ground floor, the new building contained a stair hall (with an external door), the Great Parlour and, at the north (left-hand) end, a smaller Drawing Room. The first floor contained a large ante-room linked to a bedchamber and a couple of closets.

The front has undergone a number of changes. The slate roof replaced the original covering in August 1751, when William Kilner was paid for the freight of 40 tons of Westmorland slate from Hawkshead to Cromer. The pedimented dormers are also of this date. At the same time the polygonal bay was put up at the north end and a two-storey addition for corridors added at the rear.

The Orangery

This building was contemplated as early as 1694 and it was more or less complete by 1707. Ashe Windham probably designed this austere paraphrase of the architecture of the west wing. In the 18th century, orange trees would have stood in formal patterns on the lawn in front of it during the warm weather. In the 19th century, the building was given a glass roof, which had completely rotted away by 1958, when both roof and cornice were completely reconstructed from the old drawings by R. W. Ketton-Cremer. It now contains some splendid camellias, which were planted in the 19th century.

The Interior

The Porch and Screens Passage

The Porch is spanned by a Jacobean Gothic rib vault, which has a boss displaying the Windham arms surrounded by the fetterlock (padlock) badge they took over from the Felbriggs.

Beyond lies the passage formed originally by the screen of the Jacobean Great Hall. In those days there would have been at least two doors on the right to the pantry, butteries and servery. The blank arch at the end is Jacobean.

Furniture

Four oak hall-chairs and *four walnut armchairs*, all decorated with the Windham crest, from the 1750s furnishing of the Great Hall.

Sculpture

The probably Italian, early 19th-century marble reduction of the *Farnese Hercules* was probably installed here by William Howe Windham around 1840.

The Lobby

This area, a pantry until the early 19th century, has a low ceiling like the Screens Passage, preserving an ancient mezzanine level which Thomas Wyndham of Cromer, writing in 1745, described as 'the Master's Room wch command'd the Kitchen and Hall and had for its base the Butterys. . . . No Commandant was ever better lodged in any citadel, to defend his Outworks than your Predecessors in their Metzinino between the two Halls, where meat was both dress'd and devour'd.'

Pictures

Bad pastiches of Canaletto and Van der Heyden, and naïve views of Cromer.

Bronze sculpture

Hercules with his club and an apple of the Hesperides, ? German, 17th-century. Equestrian statuette of the *Duke of Wellington* (1769–1852) by R. & S. Garrard, 1851.

Furniture

The furniture is mainly 18th-century and includes an *octagonal Neo-classical iron strong-box*, c.1780, and a *drop-leaf oval mahogany gaming-table* with spade feet, c.1780.

Ceramics

Two blue-and-white late Ming *tall cylindrical vases*, c.1640, similar to those Queen Mary used to decorate the Water Gallery, Hampton Court, c.1690. A pair of Kangxi period (1662–1722) vases and an oval blue-and-white bowl, Qianlong, late 18th-century.

The Morning Room

This was the kitchen of the Jacobean house and remained in service use until 1809, when William Collins provided designs for the 'East Parlour windows'. It was panelled out at this time and painted in tones of off-white. The present scheme may date from the mid-19th century.

Pictures

The portraits are mainly of early and mid-19th-century Windhams.

Over the chimneypiece hangs *Captain Lukin and his brothers setting off shooting, with Cawston the gamekeeper*, which was painted by William Redmore Bigg in 1803. The shooting party is setting off from Felbrigg Parsonage (now

Captain William Lukin (in the centre) and his brothers set out for a day's shooting from Felbrigg Parsonage. Lukin inherited the estate in 1824, when he changed his name to Windham; by William Redmore Bigg, 1803 (Morning Room)

demolished), where William Lukin lived until he moved into the hall in 1824. Bigg is better known as a genre painter than as an artist of sporting pictures and conversation-pieces, so the gamekeeper comes off best. Captain (later Vice-Admiral) Lukin stands in the centre, flanked by his brothers Robert and George. John, astride a horse, was later to marry the Norwich school painter John Sell Cotman and Ann Miles in Felbrigg church, seen in the distance.

Above the Lukin group is an individual portrait of *Admiral Lukin* (1768–1833), painted about 1800, before he inherited Felbrigg and changed his name to Windham. To the left are two portraits of his eldest son and heir, *William Howe Windham* (1802–54). Right of the window bay is his second son, *Captain Charles Ashe Windham* (1810–70), painted in 1833. In 1855 he led the heroic assault on the Redan in the Crimean War, and was promoted to Major-General. He tried to get his nephew William Frederick Windham certified as a lunatic.

Over the door to the Lobby is *William Frederick 'Mad' Windham* (1840–66), who inherited a heavily encumbered estate from his father, and a rogue Hervey gene from his mother. Obsessed by playing with real trains, 'Mad Windham' fell prey to an adventuress (see p. 52). His family failed to have him declared a lunatic, but the bank foreclosed. Felbrigg was bought by John Ketton, and Windham ended as an express coach-driver.

Furniture

The walnut fall-front bureau of *c.*1690 with bun feet and inlaid geometrical patterns was possibly bought by Katherine Windham in 1690/91. The *fine burr yew veneer bureau* of *c.*1720 is possibly the 'large Ewe desk with book case & glass-doors' bought in 1735 by Ashe Windham for £8 16s from Elizabeth Gumley, who continued the business founded by her son John, a famous London carver, after his death in 1727.

Ceramics

In the glazed bureau-bookcase is displayed *a service of Meissen plates and dishes* painted with birds and flowers, *c.*1755–60.

7

The Great Hall

The Great Hall of the Jacobean house, which had become by 1734 the 'common eating parlour', was entered through twin entrances in the old screen. In 1751 William Windham II made it into his neo-Tudor entrance hall with ten plaster busts on brackets and, by 1771, eighteen hall-chairs. By 1833 it had a large mahogany billiard-table.

In 1842 William Howe Windham recast the room in forceful neo-Jacobean style with heavy oak doorcases and a new ceiling with huge wooden pendants. The architects were probably G. and J. C. Buckler, and at this stage it was painted red. The present colour is post-war.

Fireplace

A Victorian design incorporating a beautiful armorial panel of the 1620s, celebrating ancient alliances. Left to right: Wyndham, Scrope, Tiptoft, Sydenham, Gambon, Wadham, Popham, Townshend, Wyndham. The stove is mid-20th-century, but the firedogs are c.1840.

Stained glass

William Howe Windham amassed the collection in the mid-19th century. It is a complex mixture of medieval and Victorian, including original panels of c.1450 removed from St Peter Mancroft, Norwich, and copies of other panels in the same church made by John Dixon in 1837. There are also fragments of medieval heraldic and religious glass made on the Continent, which Windham placed within Victorian surrounds. *A detailed handlist is available in the room.*

'Although our visit took place in May [1953] it was still far too cold to inhabit the grand suite of rooms in the west wing, so we lived and had all our meals in the Great Hall. This was heated fairly effectively by a large and ugly anthracite stove round which we sat on the few chairs that were not piled high with books.'
Brinsley Ford

Pictures

The portraits mostly depict 17th-century Windhams, their friends, relations and neighbours. They include, right of the chimneypiece, a probable portrait of *William Windham I* (1647–89), by Sir Godfrey Kneller. Flanking the door from the Screens Passage are William I's sister-in-law, *Mary Ashe* (1653–85), and her husband, *Horatio, 1st Viscount Townshend* (1630–87), who lived at nearby Raynham Hall.

Left of the chimneypiece is *Sir William Paston* (1610–62/3) of Oxnead Hall (an early 19th-century imaginary reconstruction of the house, which was demolished in the mid-18th century, hangs on the opposite wall). Paston filled Oxnead with a famous collection of works of art and curiosities. In 1638–9 he visited Egypt, where he had a brush with a crocodile, which is commemorated at the bottom left of the painting.

Right of the door to the Lobby is *Robert Wyndham Ketton-Cremer* (1906–69), the last scholar-squire of Felbrigg, who devoted his life to preserving the estate and writing about its history. The portrait was painted by Allan Gwynne-Jones in the Dining Room (where

Cleophas and St Anne; stained-glass panel, c.1450, from St Peter Mancroft, Norwich

the light is particularly good), but was left unfinished at Ketton-Cremer's death.

Sculpture

The marble 'political' busts include the great rivals of the late 18th century, William Pitt the Younger (distinguished by his pointed nose and receding chin) and Charles James Fox (stout and hairy). William Windham III – also portrayed here – was nicknamed 'weathercock Windham' for dithering in his allegiance between them. There are also marble busts of the leading military adversaries of that era, Napoleon (by Antoine-Denis Chaudet) and the Duke of Wellington (by Sir Francis Chantrey).

In the west window bay is displayed a 19th-century bronze copy of the *Laocoön*, the celebrated Antique marble rediscovered in Rome in 1506. It shows the Trojan priest Laocoön and his two sons, crushed by snakes sent by the goddess Athene for their impiety in doubting (rightly) that the wooden horse left by the Greeks was really a votive offering. *The bronze statuettes* on the table in front of the south window are also 19th-century reproductions of famous Italian statues, Giambologna's *Flying Mercury* and the Antique *Farnese Bull*.

Furniture

Against the south wall stand *walnut chairs* which were possibly intended for William Windham II's dining room of 1751. The oyster veneer *walnut cabinet* of *c.*1720 is possibly 'A walnut tree cabinet of Gumleys' bought by Ashe Windham for £10 in 1735. *The small 18th-century mahogany hanging bookcase* contains R. W. Ketton-Cremer's personal copies of his own publications. In the south bay is a *Rococo mahogany table* with marble slab, labelled 'N13 for Wm Windham Esq Felbrigg near Cromer Norfolk', 1750s.

Ceramics

French oval *blue-and-white faience cistern* painted in the Chinese manner, *c.*1700.

The Dining Room

Here you step from the Jacobean house into the west wing, which was built by William Windham I in the 1680s and wonderfully transformed by his grandson, William Windham II, into a suite of grand reception rooms. This room was formed by James Paine in 1752 out of the space previously occupied by the 1680s staircase.

Hung with portraits of William Windham II's parents and grandparents, its oval mirrors ornamented with lead chains alluding to the Windhams' fetterlock badge, it has been described as 'a Rococo evocation of a Caroline room'.

Decoration

The pale lilac is thought to be the original colour, but the dado was originally off-white and the doors were grained to resemble a dark wood (like the doors on the stairs) and would have augmented the sombre grandeur of the old portraits. The room was redecorated by Mr Dixon of Norwich in 1824; the detailed painter's bill covers plaster mouldings, doors, dadoes and window surrounds, but not the walls.

The sculpture brackets and mirrors are ornamented with lead chains – a reference to the Windhams' fetterlock badge

'The food was not as imaginative as the decoration. But it was English food at its best. And who could want anything better than lobsters from Sheringham, lamb cutlets with broad beans or peas or asparagus freshly picked from the garden, followed by gooseberry or red-currant pie with cream from the farm. The cellar was well-stocked with fine clarets and port, and given Wyndham's abstemious habits there was never any chance of it running dry.'

Brinsley Ford

Ceiling

The plasterwork was undertaken in 1752 by Joseph Rose the elder, with the assistance of George Green. The central scenes are modelled in a sinuous Rococo style, but the division into framed panels imitates the surviving 1680s ceiling of the Drawing Room. The subjects are also traditional dining-room imagery: hunting scenes in the centre, and heads symbolising the seasons in the corners – spring (with flowers), summer (ears of corn), autumn (fruit) and winter (bearded).

Fireplace

Windham had the plasterers execute Paine's design in hard stucco. The grapes and vine leaves are often found in dining rooms. The grate is mid-19th-century, but the fire-irons are c.1830.

Pictures

Over the mantelpiece is *Sir Joseph Ashe, 1st Bt* (1617/18–86), by Sir Peter Lely. He was a wealthy merchant trading with Flanders, whose financial aid to the Royalist cause earned him a baronetcy at the Restoration. His eldest daughter *Katherine* (1652–1729) married *William Windham I* (1647–89) in 1669. Their portraits flank the door to the Drawing Room. William I preferred 'ease at home, love of privacy, and good husbandry' to public life. He got William Samwell to design the west wing which contains this room, and planted quantities

of trees on the estate, particularly chestnuts. Katherine was a devoted wife, mother and grandmother, whose letters give a vivid picture of her management of Felbrigg and her family.

Right of the door from the Great Hall is William and Katherine's son and heir, *Ashe Windham* (1673–1749), painted by Sir Godfrey Kneller, before he embarked on the Grand Tour, 1693–6. At Felbrigg he built the Orangery and the service courtyard in its early form, and probably bought much of the early 18th-century furniture which remains in the house. The portrait to the left of the door may be of Ashe's wife, *Elizabeth Dobyns* (1693–1736). Married in 1709, they were soon at odds, and after the belated birth in 1717 of their only child, William Windham II, lived apart.

Kneller also painted the oval portrait over the door of Ashe's younger brother, *Col. William Windham*, MP (1674–1730), of Earsham, who lost a leg at the Battle of Blenheim (1704).

Sculpture

On the mantelpiece are (left to right) three 19th-century Italian bronze reductions of *Silenus holding the Infant Bacchus*, *The Dying Gladiator* or *Gaul*, and *Young Faun carrying a kid over his shoulders*. Left and right, above, is a pair of busts of the classical authors *Horace* and *Sappho*, supplied by John Cheere in 1752.

Furniture

Mahogany Sheraton sofa-table with satinwood banding and ebony handles, *c.*1800. *Mahogany dining-chairs* with leather seats and backs (faded now, but once green), *c.*1830, and a pair of *mahogany fireside chairs and footstools* to match. *Hepplewhite mahogany dining-table*, *c.*1790. Pair of carved *mahogany serving-tables*, *c.*1750.

Ceramics

Coalport and Ridgway dessert services, mid-19th-century.

The Drawing Room

Known until the 19th century as the 'Great Parlour', this was the main reception and dining room of the Caroline house, panelled in oak and hung with pictures. A fragment of its parquetry floor may be seen on the threshold.

It was remodelled by James Paine in 1751, retaining the original ceiling. Paine's doorcases and richly moulded dado respond to its magnificent plasterwork with spirited carving of his own time. William Windham II conceived it as a room to display the cream of his Grand Tour purchases. His marine pictures still dominate the room, but we have to try to imagine the fireplace wall in 1771 with 'Mr Dagnia painted by Shackleton' as the over-

mantel, flanked by 'An Old Usurer Rembrant' and 'Sir William Paston of the Yarmouth Family'.

Fireplace

The 1680s chimneypiece from this room is now in the Library. Its white and Siena marble successor of 1751, probably by Thomas Carter, was tried first in the Cabinet by William Windham II before finding its place here. The polished steel and brass grate is of *c*.1830.

Decoration

In 1771 the room had a flowered red paper. It was hung with the present damask by Admiral Windham *c*.1830, when the windows were given the '3 pr of splendid window curtains,

A plasterwork feast

Dated in Roman numerals 1687, this is one of the finest ceilings of its period, identical in its craftsmanship to an exactly contemporary one at Melton Constable Hall in Norfolk. Both are probably by Edward Goudge, who undertook very similar work at Belton in Lincolnshire in 1688–9. The wonderfully modelled local game birds in the corner compartments, which include pheasants, partridges, mallard, woodcocks and plovers, would have especially pleased the patron William Windham I (whose fetterlock badge may be seen near the north-west corner), as would the sprays of oak and pine cones. But there are also magnificent fruits and flowers, among them pears, grapes, quinces, apricots, lemons, almonds, pea-pods, pomegranates, roses, orange flowers and seashells. This imagery of feasting reflects the room's original purpose. In 1788 the Norwich plasterers Cato and Swain were paid for the new cornice, which is much shallower than its Caroline predecessor.

crimson damask furniture with gilt cornices, pins, drapery and holland covers'; in 1863 these and the other furnishings were protected by 'Three outside Venetian blinds'.

Furniture

The *sofa, suite of gilt chairs and fire-screens*, upholstered to match in crimson damask, were added by Admiral Windham *c.*1830. The *gilt wall-brackets* in the form of mermen, flanking the chimneypiece, and the ormolu *Rococo candle branches* above it, were made in the 1750s, originally for the Cabinet. The late 17th-century French *bureau Mazarin* is decorated with elaborate Boullework marquetry.

Furniture in 1771

'2 Large Settees, Covered with Crimson Damask, with Bolsters, 14 Mahogany chairs, With Crimson Damask Bottoms and Red and White Check Covers to the Setees and Chairs, a Very fine India Screen, With Six Leaves' and 'a Very Large Turkey Carpet' [the chairs and sofas are now in the Stone Corridor, West Corridor and Great Hall].

Pictures

Over the chimneypiece is *William Windham III* (1750–1810), a copy by John Jackson after Sir Thomas Lawrence's original of 1803. He was the last of the true Windhams of Felbrigg, its only owner to perform upon the national stage, diarist and friend of Samuel Johnson. He served as belligerent Secretary at War in Pitt's Cabinet from 1794 to 1801. In 1798 he finally married Cecilia Forrest, after a long-standing platonic affair with her sister Bridget. Resigning with Pitt in 1801, he was Secretary for War and the Colonies in Grenville's 'Ministry of all the Talents' in 1806–7. He saw himself as 'a scholar among politicians and a politician among scholars'. The portrait conceals the fact that his face was badly scarred by smallpox.

Sir Joshua Reynolds's portrait of *George Cholmondeley* (1752–1830) hangs to the left of the chimneypiece. It was painted for William Windham III, in exchange for a portrait of

(Below)   The Battle of the Texel (1673); by Willem van de Velde the Elder and Younger

Windham by Reynolds (now in the National Portrait Gallery). Cholmondeley was his closest friend, and Windham at one point made a will leaving Felbrigg to him and then to Cholmondeley's eldest son by his mistress, Cecilia Forrest, whom Windham was ultimately himself to marry.

William Windham II's *big marine and topographical views* still dominate the end walls. He 'could and did build vessels, and navigate them himself', according to his friend Richard Aldworth.

Flanking the door to the Dining Room are Willem van de Velde the Elder's two depictions of *The Battle of the Texel* (1673). Texel was the last major sea fight of the three Anglo-Dutch wars, in which the Dutch admiral De Ruyter thwarted the English commander-in-chief Prince Rupert's attempt to draw out and destroy his fleet, in order to make way for a joint invasion of Holland with the French.

The picture on the left shows the crucial episode of the battle, when Cornelis Tromp's flagship, the *Gouden Leeuw* (Golden Lion),

Old London Bridge; by Samuel Scott, 1753. The houses on the bridge were pulled down four years after the picture was painted

bombarded the *Royal Prince*, the flagship of Admiral Sir Edward Spragge, so severely that the latter was forced to abandon it. Kindly lent back to the house by the National Maritime Museum, to which Ketton-Cremer had sold it in 1934.

The picture on the right shows a somewhat later moment, just before Spragge transferred his flag from the *Royal Prince* (in the left foreground, with only her foremast standing) to the *St George* (at the left with a blue flag at the main); close to starboard of the *Prince* is the *Gouden Leeuw*.

Left of the door to the Cabinet is Samuel Scott's **Old London Bridge**. Scott painted this subject no fewer than eleven times, first in 1747, the year after the Lord Mayor had called a Court of Enquiry to consider the future of the bridge, which was a dangerous obstacle to traffic on the Thames. (This version was painted in 1753.) The houses on it were pulled down, and a single central arch built, in 1757, but the rest of the bridge was not demolished until 1831.

Right of the door is Samuel Scott's **The Thames by the Tower of London.**

Carpet

An 'English Savonnerie' design of *c*.1851.

Ceramics

New Hall **teapot** given by Queen Mary. Series of **Meissen dishes** painted with flowers, *c*.1755–60. Pair of large mid-19th-century Chinese *famille rose* **hexagonal vases**. On the chimneypiece stands a pair of French late 18th-century biscuit *figure groups*, signed 'Constant'.

Clock

Bracket clock in ebonised case by John Martin of London, 18th-century.

The Thames by the Tower of London; by Samuel Scott

The Cabinet

This was built as the 'Drawing Room' of the 1680s wing (the room to which family and guests would withdraw after meals in the adjacent Great Parlour). It was square in plan and panelled until the bay window was added in 1751, when William Windham II remodelled the room as the setting for the Italian pictures which he had acquired on the Grand Tour.

The Grand Tour

During the 18th century, rich young Englishmen often finished their education by touring the Continent. They usually took in the historic cities of Italy, including Rome, where they could absorb the greatest works of classical and Renaissance art at first hand. For some, it was merely an excuse for a drunken binge, but others, like William Windham II, took the journey more seriously, refining their critical faculties and acquiring paintings, sculpture and furniture to decorate their homes back in Britain.

Ceiling

The square plaster ceiling of c.1687 survives; its plan is similar to that over the staircase at Belton, which Edward Goudge was to execute in 1688–9. The Rococo filling of the central panel, the delicately modelled cove with its trails of flowers and the arms of Windham and his wife Sarah Hicks, and the ceiling of the bay were designed by Paine and put up by George Green with the assistance of John Wegg, between October 1750 and January 1751. Cato and Swaine's bill for '90 feet of Enrich'd Cornice in Bow Drawing Room' of 1788 may refer to the dentil cornice.

Fireplace

The marble surround and the polished steel grate were made by the Norwich mason John Blackburn in 1789. The richly carved central plaque was supplied by a London carver. This ensemble replaced a chimneypiece supplied in July 1752 by Thomas Carter which appears to have been decorated with flowers.

Decoration

The hangings and the gilded cord edging had been ordered in 1751. The crimson worsted damask is remarkably well preserved and the size of its single repeat, which runs very nearly from cornice to chair rail, is unusual. The gilt cornice and pelmet over the window belong to curtains introduced by Admiral Windham c.1830.

Furniture

The *gilded overmantel mirror and picture frame* were ordered from John Bladwell in March 1752. The splendid *Rococo pier-table* was made by a leading London craftsman, perhaps James Whittle or Thomas Chippendale. The Siena marble top was supplied by Thomas Carter. The pair of *ormolu candle branches* matches the pair in the Drawing Room, like the two *gilded plaster wall-brackets* flanking the window bay, which represent Apollo and, possibly, Daphne, and have been attributed to John Cheere. The French-style upholstered *mahogany chairs* with carved cabriole legs of c.1750 were partly upholstered in red damask by Admiral Windham for his Drawing Room.

One of the four *giltwood torchères* bears the label of William Freeman of Norwich, c.1830 (the Neo-classical candlesticks are contemporary).

Furnishings in 1771

'2 Large Mahogany Settees, carved and covered with Crimson Damask. 2 Bolsters to Each. 10 Large Mahogany arm Chairs Covered with Crimson Damask. 3 Stools of the same and Covers to all of Crimson Baize.' The legs and arms were carved with Chinoiserie lattice and the seat rails were scalloped. Nearly all the original 1750s furniture of the Cabinet was disposed of in 1918.

Pictures

The Cabinet has long been celebrated as the epitome of the Grand Tour, an almost unique, virtually intact survival of an 18th-century collection made on such a tour, hung as the collector himself planned it, the very drawings for which, drawn up to Windham's instructions by Paine's foreman, Hull, and annotated by him, still exist in the archive.

The hang was conceived in tandem with that of the Drawing Room, as the matching character of the different Rococo patterns of the frames (probably by René Duffour) in the two rooms indicate. It was carried out in 1752–3, with Windham himself present, as he had insisted to his steward, Frary. In the Drawing Room, marines and naval engagements set the tone, but landscape and topography complement these; in the Cabinet, the proportions are reversed, and, amongst the landscapes, a very special place is given to six large oils and 26 little gouaches of Rome and its environs by Giovanni Battista Busiri, known as 'Titarella' (1698–1757), for which Windham evidently had an especial predilection, and that he had acquired or ordered when in Rome in 1739 (they are variously dated 1739 or 1740).

Many of the gouaches are of classic sites, but with a preference for bridges, tombs and other Antique ruins standing in nature, for Windham evidently had a particular fondness for the Roman Campagna itself.

Ceramics

The two Dehua *blanc-de-Chine* **libation cups**, late 17th- or early 18th-century, are based on rhinoceros horn originals.

Clock

Fourteen-day striking mantel clock in ormolu and marble case, signed 'De Belle, Rue St Honoré, A Paris', *c.*1790. The white marble base, incorporating an aneroid barometer and two thermometers, was added *c.*1870.

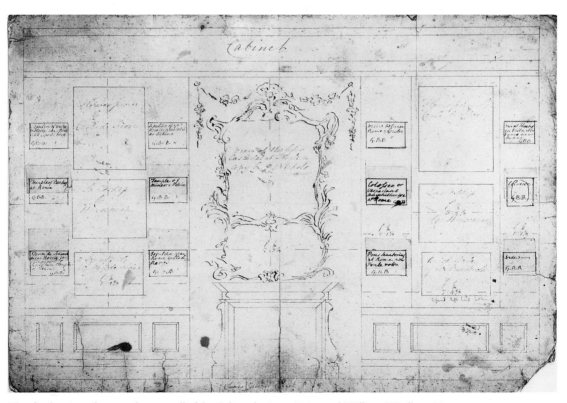

Plan for the picture hang on the east wall of the Cabinet by James Paine and William Windham II

A Bridge near Tivoli called Ponte del' Aqua Auria; By G. B. Busiri. One of 32 views of Rome and its surroundings acquired by William Windham II while in Rome in 1739 or shortly afterwards

Chandelier
Crystal gasolier, later 19th-century.

Carpet
William Windham II's Wilton carpet was replaced *c.*1851 by the present 'English Savonnerie' carpet.

The Stone Corridor

This and the West Corridor above are an extension built by William Windham II in 1751–2. The 18th-century decoration is not known, but in the later 19th century this, like other service corridors and attic stairs, was painted a rich red. The present scheme is modern.

Furniture
The *walnut chairs* with simple pierced splats in two patterns were probably in the Dining Room in 1771. The series of fine *mahogany chairs* with scroll-pattern backs in the style of Robert Mainwaring may have been in the Great Parlour (now Drawing Room) in 1771.

Ceramics and glass
The Sheraton-style cabinet displays a collection of *mid-18th-century glasses*, as well as late 18th-century *Chinese export porcelain*. Of particular interest are two *chamberpots*, one Chinese, *c.*1720, the other with flowers, Boisette, *c.*1780.

Clock
Eight-day longcase clock by Thomas Church of Norwich, mid-18th-century.

> 'I think it was generally agreed that Felbrigg was one of the coldest houses in England.'
>
> Brinsley Ford

The Stair Hall

The construction of James Paine's Stair Hall was begun in the spring of 1752. It occupied much of the site of the 1680s stairs, but actually achieved fewer and more gradual flights in a smaller space. Paine's design, for which the drawing survives, was closely related to his Dining Room and Great Hall in its use of plaster decoration and bronzed plaster casts. It included a timber and plaster barrel vault, lit at either end by semicircular 'therm' windows. This exerted too much thrust on the side walls and was replaced in 1813 by Humphry Repton and his son John Adey with a more conventional sky-light (subsequently removed).

In June 1752 Windham cancelled the medals which had been made to go over the north doors on the gallery in favour of two more busts. That is why the *rocaille* brackets are different from the rest. In the same month ale was given to the stonecutters to celebrate the completion of the floor here and in the Stone Corridor. The plasterwork seems to have been finished by November, but it was not until June 1753 that Thomas Wagg, described by Windham as 'a top master-workman' who 'lives in a very good way', was able to install his beautiful iron balustrading.

Decoration

The Stair Hall was redecorated for Admiral Windham in 1824 by Dixon of Norwich. There is a general resemblance to Paine's Dining Room scheme, but with less attractive colours.

Pictures

Most of the portraits here came from Beeston Regis, the Norfolk seat of the Cremer family from the 18th to the 20th centuries. However, they are not a coherent group, and none is inscribed. Indeed it is perfectly possible that they came with, and depict, members of the Green and Woodrow families, and of others with which the Cremers had also intermarried.

There are also two big full-lengths:

'Count' James Dagnia (*c.*1708/9–55), painted by John Shackleton, is a mysterious figure. He was from a family of glass manufacturers of Italian origin who had settled at Cleadon, Co. Durham, where his father had bought an estate and built Cleadon Hall. Known as 'the famous gentleman glassblower' and 'the gentleman painter', he figured as 'Count Dagnia' in Rome, where he was much patronised by English noblemen, and where it is probable that his friendship with William Windham II was formed.

Dagnia may have painted *William Windham II* (1717–61) *as a young man in the costume of a Hussar.* This portrait seems to have given rise to the legend that, when on his travels (1738–42), Windham served as an officer in the Empress Maria Theresa's regiment of Hungarian Hussars. This is inherently improbable, but the complete nature of his costume here suggests more than fancy dress, and that he actually possessed the real thing. It may be another indication that he did get as far as Vienna and Hungary. After Maria Theresa's coronation as Queen of Hungary in 1741, the Hungarians became her stoutest defenders, and the Hussars popular symbols of this for her English allies.

Sculpture

The busts in bronzed plaster on brackets in the blank oculi are real or imagined likenesses of Ancient Greeks and Romans by John Cheere (like those in the Dining Room).

Furniture

The armchair and two side-chairs of *c.*1690 beneath the stairs are among the earliest pieces in the house and were probably acquired by Katherine Windham. The chairs on the half-landing and gallery are Chinese Chippendale, *c.*1750.

Clocks

At the foot of the stairs is an eight-day longcase clock by John Snow of London in a Chinese lacquer case, *c.*1730. On the gallery is an eight-day striking clock by Joseph Herring of London in a Chinese lacquer case, *c.*1750.

Lantern

Possibly the one listed in the Great Hall in 1771.

The Library

This was probably the Great Chamber of the Jacobean house and was made into the Library by William Windham II in 1752–5. Windham's object was to house the books which he had bought on the Grand Tour as well as those of his father and grandfather. He settled on a Gothic interior, considered appropriate to the character of the old south front.

Paine's oak bookcases were being finished by George Church in January 1755. The old west bay window was blocked and shelved up in 1787 by William Windham III, who needed more space for his books. At this time it appears that the panels of tracery decoration, based on the design of the 1750s library table (see below), were added to the presses. The architect of these changes was Robert Furze Brettingham.

Fireplace

The veined marble bolection-moulded surround of *c.*1685 came originally from the Caroline Great Parlour and was moved here because, as Windham wrote in January 1752, 'It is of bilection work more in the old taste'. The grate and dogs are mid-19th-century, as is the oak overmantel.

Books

A number of volumes survive from the time of William Windham I and his son Ashe. William's are identifiable by his fine armorial bookplate. In one of her notebooks, his wife Katherine listed her books, which included a stout volume of plays by Dryden, Otway, Wycherley and other contemporary dramatists, which still remains in the library. Other works from this

Re-creating the ceiling

In 1924, after years of neglect, the Ketton-Cremers were forced to take down the ceiling, with its neo-Jacobean fret of squares and octagons, because of the damage caused by a leaking roof. Unfortunately, they could afford to replace it only with a plain flat ceiling.

R. W. Ketton-Cremer had always hoped that Paine's full ceiling design of 1752 might be re-created. Following the discovery of surviving plasterwork from the blocked-up west bay during repair work in 1999, the decision was taken in 2000 to do this. The re-created scheme drew on all the available evidence, including Paine's sketch, two late 19th-century photographs of the room and a section of original plaster. The plasterwork was undertaken by Stevensons of Norwich using traditional methods and materials, with the fretwork being composed both of elements run *in situ* and pre-cast elements made off-site.

early period include manuals of piety such as *The Whole Duty of Man*, or more practical volumes on medicine, cookery and gardening, including Evelyn's *Sylva*.

William Windham II formed the core of the collection now at Felbrigg. His interests in architecture, the sciences and languages are reflected in his purchases. Many of the large folios on architecture and classical antiquities were bought on his prolonged Grand Tour of 1738–42. While in Geneva he acquired a copy of Gauffecourt's *Traité de la reliure*, and he also owned a large outfit of binders' tools and materials (see p. 29). Around 300 volumes of miscellaneous pamphlets containing poems, plays, scientific and mathematical treatises were probably bound on the premises under his supervision. Quite a few still include instructions to a binder in his hand. Besides being an avid reader, Windham was himself the author of a number of pamphlets, ranging from a lively squib against Smollett's translation of *Don Quixote* to an immensely elaborate training manual, *A Plan of Discipline* (1759), for the county militia. Another rarity is the manuscript of *Ragandjaw*, a short satirical play written by David Garrick and dedicated to Windham in 1746.

William Windham III added greatly to his father's collection of books, particularly in the fields of literature, philosophy, politics and economics. Still to be found here are Dr Johnson's own copies of the *Iliad*, *Odyssey* and New Testament, which he inherited from his friend, with eighteen other volumes bought at the sale of Johnson's effects in 1785. Apart from Windham's own early diaries, edited by R. W. Ketton-Cremer, two volumes of particular interest are Nathaniel Kent's agricultural treatises of 1775 and 1796, based to a large extent on his management and planting of the Felbrigg estate on Windham's behalf.

Comparatively few books were added to the collection by Admiral Lukin or his son William Howe Windham, described as a 'rough unlettered squire'. The bulk of modern collecting activity can be found in the working library of R. W. Ketton-Cremer, most of which is now at the University of East Anglia.

Furniture

The mahogany *library table* with drawers and tracery decoration is one of two made to Paine's design by George Church in 1753 for £21. The *celestial and terrestrial globes* on satinwood veneer stands were made by J. & W. Cary of 181 The Strand, in 1799 and 1814 respectively.

The Book Room

Entered through a concealed jib-door in one of the presses, this was Sarah Windham's bedroom in the 1750s, and, as the 1771 inventory records, had an embroidered bed lined with green silk, a suite of seat furniture covered in green damask with green and white checked case covers and 'a Large Mahogany Case for China or Books' (now in the Stair Hall), as well as a 'Ewe Tree Bureau with Looking Glass Doors' (now in the Morning Room). The walls were hung with green flowered paper and the adjacent 'light closet' furnished with two damask-covered stools and a mahogany table.

All this was changed in the 1780s when William Windham III turned this into a convenient sitting room. The diarist Joseph Farington records, 'The Library is upstairs, and in a room adjoining it Mr Windham always sat when engaged in business or study.... During this time he slept in a small tent bed put up in a niche in a room next to His sitting room, for the convenience of it being near the Library.' The Gothic plaster frieze, probably designed by Robert Brettingham, dates from this period.

Pictures

The picture-hang here changes periodically to show works from the rest of the collection. Around the walls is a variety of drawings and watercolours of Norfolk and – in particular – Felbrigg, ranging from the 18th to the 20th centuries, and mostly signed or labelled.

Furniture

The display cabinets and bookcases were designed by John Bedford and made by Daniel Windham.

The Grey Dressing Room

The door to the Grey Dressing Room brings us back into the 1680s wing. Its angled entrance results from the projection of one of the Jacobean hall chimneystacks. In order to create a rectangular plan, Paine reduced the size of the room, allowing generous storage space in the embrasure.

The Grey Dressing Room

This modest room, panelled out by George Church in 1753, was used by William Windham II as his dressing room.

Furniture

The fine *Rococo mirror* of *c.*1750, now painted grey, was probably supplied by John Bladwell.

The Yellow Bedroom

This was 'The Green Bedchamber' in 1771 with a crimson and green silk damask bed, walnut chairs with matching seats, curtains of green lutestring (a glossy silk) and a flowered green wallpaper. Like the Grey Dressing Room, it was formed out of the old Stair Hall and all the architectural detail is of 1752–3.

Decoration

The room was repainted in the 1970s to re-create a 1920s scheme of R. W. Ketton-Cremer's parents.

Pictures

To the right of the door to the Rose Bedroom hangs a pastel portrait of *William Windham II* (1717–61) *as a young man*, which was painted by Barthélémy du Pan, probably in Geneva, where Windham was from 1738 to 1742.

Jan van Kessel's *A bleaching-ground outside Haarlem* shows the grounds near van Kessel's native town, where laundry was left to be dried and bleached by the sun.

The Rose Bedroom

This room appears to have been first fitted out in 1705. The dado panelling is of that time, if somewhat reorganised, and so is the timber cornice. The doors are of an early 18th-century pattern. Two are modern copies of doors which found their way into Donthorn's stables. The two beside the fireplace are original.

Ceiling

The plaster cove and border seem to contain elements by Edward Goudge of *c.*1687, but it is probable that they were all salvaged from the Great Stairs ceiling and rearranged here by *c.*1752–3 by George Green, who showed such facility in manipulating the Caroline plasterwork in the Cabinet. There are noticeable differences in design and workmanship, especially between the garlands over the fireplace wall, suspended

The Rose Bedroom

from rings and hooks, as opposed to the knots of drapery used in the other coves. The border of laurel and oak is also reused 1680s work.

Pictures

Left of the bed, the pencil sketch of *William Windham III making his maiden speech in Norwich in 1778* was drawn by the future landscape gardener Humphry Repton, who began his career as Windham's political secretary. Windham entered politics by speaking at a public meeting in Norwich against the war with the American colonies. He is shown holding the petition he drew up after the meeting.

Furniture

The *mahogany half-tester bed, wash-stand, dressing-table, wardrobe and window cornices* are all *c.*1840. The two white and gilt *pier-glasses* of *c.*1752 were made by John Bladwell to accommodate late 17th-century bevelled mirror glass. The two mahogany cupboards of *c.*1820 were used to conceal chamberpots. The large *sofa* with serpentine back and two upholstered *side-chairs* of *c.*1750 are part of the same suite.

Colours revived

In 2004 the National Trust replaced all the printed rose chintz and lining fabric, including the bed-hangings, window curtains and pelmets, and loose covers for the sofa and two chairs. The original 1840s fabric had dramatically faded, losing most of the red and green colour of the rose pattern. The replica fabric is an exact copy, specially reproduced using traditional printing techniques. It shows the depth of colour of the original, found in a small area of unfaded material at the bottom of one curtain.

The Red Bedroom

Here the dado panelling and cornice are of
c.1705 and the former noticeably more elaborate
than in the Rose Bedroom. In 1771 this had
become a well-appointed bedchamber with
flowered grey wallpaper.

Decoration

The room was last decorated c.1860. The rich
flock and gilt wallpaper is of this period but has
lost much of its colour. The buff stripes were
once candy pink. The gilt cord survives from
the 1750s decoration.

Furniture

The fine *Rococo gilt pier-glass* of c.1752, by John
Bladwell, has 17th-century glass. The *overmantel
mirror*, c.1752, resembles one of Paine's designs
for a fireplace at Felbrigg. In September 1751
Windham wrote, 'I find it is a high fashion for
oval glasses to be placed over chimneys, and
carved work around them.' The *reclining chair*,
manufactured by John Carter c.1850, is
described on its label as a 'Literary Machine' and
was, it seems, made for the Library.

The Red Bedroom

The Chinese Bedroom

A mid-18th-century plan of the house shows
this room divided into two. In 1751 the bay
window was built by William Windham II,
and the two rooms united by James Paine,
who nonetheless retained the late 17th-
century form of coved ceiling. It was described
as the 'Bow Window Dressing Room' in 1771,
when the Chinese paper hangings would have
harmonised beautifully with the white and
grey scheme in the adjacent room, which
it served.

Furniture

The *mahogany bed*, c.1830, has two posts of
c.1750. The chintz hangings are of the later
period and match those in the Red Bedroom.
The *small Chinese Coromandel lacquer cabinet*
on a fine mid-18th-century English stand is
probably the 'Small Elegant India Cabinet in
Colours' described in 1771 in what is now the
Yellow Bedroom. The *mahogany dressing-table
glass* of c.1790 incorporates cut mirror glass of
c.1700.

The West Corridor

Built in 1751–2 to provide service access to
the new bedrooms of the west wing. The water
closet at the north end was added by Robert
Brettingham in 1788 (see also the Stone
Corridor beneath).

Sculpture

The *bronzed plaster bust* is of the poet
Alexander Pope (1688–1744) by John Cheere
after Roubiliac.

Furniture

The *fall-front, walnut-veneer escritoire* (writing-
desk), c.1690, is possibly one bought by
Katherine Windham in 1690/91. The handles
and feet were replaced c.1715. The six handsome *mahogany chairs* of c.1750 with scroll-
pattern splats probably came from William
Windham II's Great Parlour. The *mahogany
military chest* of c.1800 with carrying handles is
thought to have been used on naval service by

Agnes Willoughby, who married 'Mad Windham' for his money in 1861, made clear that she would not move to Felbrigg unless an enamel bath with hot and cold water laid on was installed. But Wyndham Ketton-Cremer states that there were no bathrooms when his parents moved in, 'since Robert Ketton had remained faithful to the hip-bath all his days'.

Admiral Windham. The *walnut veneer bureau* of *c*.1730–40 is doubtless the 'Large Cabinet with Draws Finered, and with a Looking Glass Door' listed in 1771 in the Tapestry Room (over the Morning Room). The *Victorian papier-mâché trays* were made by Clay of King Street, Covent Garden.

Lighting

The *glass bowls* on brass pillars are candle shades. The mahogany stands are also for candles and are frequently listed in conjunction with dressing-tables in the 1771 inventory.

The Bathroom

This room was probably turned into a bathroom by the Ketton-Cremers in the 1920s. The pictorial designs of its early linoleum suggest that it may previously have been used in a nursery.

Furniture

The *Chinese Coromandel lacquer screen* of *c*.1700 and the *red lacquer bureau* of *c*.1730 are both important early pieces.

The Back Stairs

The 1680s wing had a service staircase in this area, but the present stairs were built in the autumn of 1751. The present balusters are of a late 17th-century type identical to those on the great stairs at Aylsham Old Hall, completed *c*.1686. They must therefore have been salvaged from the demolition of the Felbrigg Great Stairs.

The Bird Corridor

Built by Admiral Windham in 1831 to improve communication between the Kitchen and Dining Room, this encloses the windows of earlier rooms in the extension built in 1675. In 1734 the first two windows lit the 'Common Drawing Room' (since 1787 the Butler's Pantry), the central one relates to the secondary staircase and in 1734 the furthest window lit the Housekeeper's Room (since *c*.1750 the China Room).

Taxidermy

The collection of Thomas Wyndham Cremer (1834–94), the last squire's grandfather, who was a keen ornithologist. The set-ups are by Gunn of Norwich and Pratt of Brighton.

A figure from a very important Athenian grave monument of 350–20 BC. Part of a large relief which would have included a standing figure on the left-hand side, who was, to judge by other contemporary monuments, probably clasping the seated lady's right hand. It was first recorded at Felbrigg in the Walled Garden in 1847 and described as 'A mutilated white marble statue, lately dug up on the plains of Troy'. The figure is a close contemporary of the Elgin Marbles and it may be significant that Philip Hunt, who as chaplain to the Earl of Elgin encouraged the removal of the Parthenon sculptures to England, ended his days as vicar of nearby Aylsham in 1838.

The Butler's Pantry

This room, which may be viewed through a pane in the second window on the right, seems to have been fitted out c.1787 and was presumably therefore designed by Robert Furze Brettingham for William Windham III. Its cupboarded walls would have housed the large quantity of glassware for which the butler was responsible.

The China Room

This room, visible through a pane in the fourth window on the right, was fitted out c.1750 with oak cupboards on its east wall and small shelves ranged round the fireplace. Tiled like the one in the Grey Dressing Room, it was fitted with a stove, and now contains a collection of late 18th-century blue-and-white plates, bowls and meat dishes.

Copper in the Kitchen

Love panes

Scratched into one of the lower panes of the China Room is a verse written in praise of a local beauty, Anne Barnes, by her devoted admirer Benjamin Stillingfleet, William Windham II's tutor:

Could Lammy look within my breast
She'd find her image there exprest
In characters as deep as here
The letters of her name appear
And like them ever will remain
Till time shall break my heart in twain.

It is signed 'B. Stillingfleet, fool'. His persistent suit eventually foundered on his lack of income and prospects in 1735 and provoked a *Philippic against Woman*.

The Kitchen

The Kitchen has occupied this site since the early 18th century, but its ceiling was raised probably c.1800, when the two round-headed windows were made in its east wall. The charcoal stove between them is also of this date, but it appears that the old range was removed by the last squire, who introduced the present Aga.

Furniture

One of the *large oak tables* is 18th-century, the other Victorian. The *large oak cupboard*, now painted, but originally intended for a more polite room, was made c.1730 and extended at the back in pine and given a new cornice c.1800.

Pewter

A series of *large 18th-century chargers*, two of which are engraved on their rims with the Windham fetterlock crest.

Next to the Kitchen are the doors to the Housekeeper's Room and the Still Room.

The South Corridor

The new west service wing was built by James Paine for William Windham II in 1749–51 to contain a new Servants' Hall, Steward's Room, a Tenants' Waiting Room and a group of workshops. It had lodging rooms on the first floor and an open arcaded walk at the front, which was turned into a corridor by W. J. Donthorn in 1825 for Admiral Windham. The colour schemes here and throughout the wing are based on analysis of paint samples which are thought to represent the early 19th-century decoration. They were undertaken in 1993.

The *fire buckets* bear the initials of Rachel Anne Ketton which must have been applied between 1872 (the death of her husband John Ketton) and 1875 (the majority of their son Robert). The leather ones are probably 18th-century, and their purchase was the subject of anxious letters from the agent Robert Thurston after the explosion of the firework shop in 1755. The *house fire-engine* was probably provided in the late 18th century.

Furniture

The *cupboard with Gothic details* is a press provided for William Windham II's library by George Church *c*.1755.

The Servants' Hall

Before the building of the wing, the Servants' Hall was in the west service range. Francis Pank was paid for the floor and ceiling here in November 1749, and George Church received payment 'For fitting up the Servants Hall making the tables benches . . . etc.'. Church's benches and tables remain in the room.

The Steward's Room

The estate was administered from this room until 1970. Church fitted it out in March–May 1750 and probably also made the *oak desk*.

Pictures

Sheringham Beach was painted by Charles Catton the Younger in 1794. Ketton-Cremer remembered his father saying that 'the figure with the dog and crook (though it is perhaps less like a crook than a boat hook) represents the Shepherd employed at Beeston by my Great Great Grandfather, Cremer Cremer (died 1808), who presumably ordered the picture'.

Surveying wheel

This early 19th-century device for measuring distances has a dial calibrated in yards, poles, furlongs and miles, and is marked 'M. Berge, London'. William Windham II was interested in these devices.

The Tenants' Waiting Room

This room was fitted out by Church in December 1749, but the cupboards at the east end are probably early 19th-century.

The Turnery

This was one of William Windham II's two wood-turning shops; the other one was overhead. George Church set up the 'turns' in November 1750, and an inventory made about 1755 lists an impressive array of chisels, differential chucks and other items relating to turning, which was a popular 18th-century hobby. Windham had a large range of wood, both hard and soft, as well as ivory, tortoiseshell and amber, and had produced at the time of the inventory some little boxes in yew and *lignum vitae*, as well as different types of spinning top. The shops also stored Windham's arsenal of sporting arms. There were 42 different guns in the upper shop alone, as well as Geneva bows, crossbows, bullet-bows, an Indian ironwood bow and a Madagascar lance. The upper shop, which was hung with prints and maps, also contained Windham's bookbinding and gilding tools. In addition, the shops were used for general joinery work, and contained tools for working iron and brass, for watchmaking and gun repair.

The Garden

The gentle south-facing slope, a slightly acid soil and the protection afforded by the Great Wood provide good conditions for gardening at Felbrigg in spite of its notoriously severe climate. Annual average rainfall is 22 inches.

The American Garden

The garden north of the house and around the Orangery was probably remodelled by Broderick Thomas, who provided a plan in June 1865 for the new owner John Ketton. Many of the trees are of transatlantic origin, notably the American Buckeye (*Aesculus parviflora*) – hence the garden's name. There are also Red Oaks (*Quercus rubra*), False Acacia (*Robinia pseudoacacia*) and the Tulip Tree, *Liriodendron tulipiferum*. Wellingtonias (*Sequoiadendron giganteum*) adjoin the Orangery, where they are accompanied by Evergreen Oaks (*Quercus ilex*) and a fine group of the large flowering broom, *Genista aetnensis*, next to the path. The remarkable curving trunks of the Western Red Cedars (*Thuja plicata*) make an impressive prelude to the walk which leads to the Walled Garden. It is an altogether typical Victorian pleasure ground, and in recent years the Trust has added spring-flowering rhododendrons and azaleas, bamboo and the flowering privet, *Ligustrum lucidum*.

The Walled Garden

It is not known when this garden was begun, though William Windham II contributed its most distinctive feature, the octagonal Dove-house, in the early 1750s. The east and west walls were rebuilt by Admiral Windham in 1825 according to the plaque above the entrance. A plan of the garden was made for William Howe Windham in 1834, following the Admiral's death. Grigor's *Eastern Arboretum* of

1847 recorded, 'The Kitchen Garden here is well worthy of notice. It is exceedingly well kept. Through the exertions of Mr Robins of pine growing celebrity, it has been raised to a style of excellence which few gardens present.' W. H. Windham enhanced the ornamental character of the garden, especially of the Dove-house Walk, by introducing the central circular pond and in 1842 the old front-door arch of the hall. The two stone pine-cones on the gateway near the entrance are finials from the roof of the 1680s west wing, taken down in the repairs of 1751. The other smaller pine-cone is a later copy.

During Felbrigg's decline in the early 20th century the Walled Garden was leased out to a market gardener, but there was no investment in the care of its glasshouses. When the last squire's parents took over the property in 1923, they were able to repair only the two main houses on either side of the Dove-house Walk.

The entrance to the garden is flanked by two Irish yews (*Taxus baccata* 'Fastigiata'), planted to match the more mature specimens at the opposite end of the central path, which is defined by the box hedging for which the garden is well known. The gate-piers on the west walk are clad with sweet bays (*Laurus nobilis*) and myrtles (*Myrtus communis*). Only the north-east section of the garden is still used for vegetables, but the walls are well stocked with plums, pears, apples, figs and gages, peaches and nectarines.

The herb borders lie to the east and west of the Dove-house and have become a special feature of the garden during the last decade. The other beds beneath the walls are planted as mixed borders with roses, paeonies, hibiscus, phlox and dahlias. Dahlias were the dominant feature of the central path in the last squire's time but these double borders were redesigned in 1977 by John Sales, the Trust's former Gardens Adviser, with a variety of shrubs to provide colour and interest throughout the summer. Planted in front of these in the shelter of the box hedges is *Colchicum tenorei*, which has become the focus for a National Collection of the genus.

The Greenhouses

These symmetrical houses appear on the 1834 plan. One is a vinery with a good specimen of 'Black Hamburgh' and also contains a grapefruit tree which fruits regularly. The other is a conservatory for flowering plants, dominated by a large mimosa (*Acacia dealbata*). They were repaired in 2004.

Near the small propagating house in the north-west section is a Californian Bay (*Umbellularia californica*) known, because of its powerfully scented foliage, as the headache tree. A good collection of large old-fashioned roses occupies the plot behind, and others may be seen on the nearby lawn. Either side of the central path are 'Norfolk Royal Russet' apples trained as dwarf pyramids. The orchard area is left uncut until late summer to allow the wild flowers to seed.

The lawns in the central section were replanted with olive trees in 2004. The South Lawn is treated as an open area with attractive cream- and yellow-flowered climbing roses and various forms of ceanothus on its sunny north wall.

The Dove-house

The present octagon was probably built in 1753. In 1923 it was 'almost a ruin, with gaping holes in the roof, the principal timbers rotted through, and the cupola

(Right) The Dove-house

leaning drunkenly awry'. It was restored by Wyndham Ketton-Cremer in 1937, as the Latin inscription records. Dove-houses were an important source of meat in the past, and the young birds, or squabs, would be collected for the kitchen from the numerous nesting holes.

The South Garden

This garden, in front of the east wing, was laid out in memory of Wyndham Ketton-Cremer. Its box-edged beds contain *Rosa rugosa* 'Fru Dagmar Hastrup', and Rose 'Nevada' and 'Little White Pet'. On the south wall of the wing is a fine wisteria and a *Garrya elliptica*.

The Estate and Park

The estate which Wyndham Ketton-Cremer bequeathed to the National Trust in 1969 consisted of 2,180 acres (881 hectares), of which about a quarter was to be regarded as alienable so that sales could be put towards the endowment. Since then 425 acres of alienable land have been sold; the estate now stands at 1,755 acres (709 hectares).

The nucleus of this estate was built up before the Norman Conquest and enlarged by the Felbrigg family to include a detached holding at Tuttington. When Sir John Wyndham acquired Felbrigg in about 1450, he brought with him substantial lands at Wicklewood and Crownthorpe, and this holding was increased by his successors, Sir Thomas and Sir Edmund Wyndham, to include land at Sustead and Metton as well as the former monastic property of Beeston Priory.

In 1665 William Windham I began an epoch of enterprising direct management whose details were carefully recorded in the famous Green Book (see p. 38). Against a background of tumbling corn prices and declining profit margins on fat stock and dairy, however, William Windham's energy succeeded only in averting decline. The increasing wealth which he enjoyed arose from the clever investment of surplus capital in mortgages and loans. His widow Katherine managed Felbrigg herself from 1689 to 1694, during which time so many tenants gave up in the face of economic recession that she found herself farming nearly half the estate.

The next creative phase was under the aegis of William Windham III, who in 1775 put the estate in the hands of a professional, Nathaniel Kent. With his advice Windham skilfully enclosed much of the common land in the parish, leaving the villagers the least fertile parts of the heath for the gathering of wood. Felbrigg became a test bed for Kent's theories on the management of timber. He published *Hints to Gentlemen of Landed Property* in 1775, when he had just set about the reorganisation of the woods, and was able to confirm the success of his measures in *A General View of the Agriculture of Norfolk* in 1796. It was at this time that many

The tenants of Park Wall Farm in the late 19th century

of the peripheral tree belts were planted and that the general appearance of the park today was established. William Marshall's *Rural Economy of Norfolk*, published in 1787, held up Felbrigg as a model of good management.

The estate reached its largest extent under the improving landlord William Howe Windham, whose initialled date stones bear witness to the great number of farm buildings which he erected or improved throughout the area. In 1854 there were 7,000 acres at Felbrigg together with the newly acquired Hanworth Estate of 1,500 acres, 600 at Alby and a further 1,000 at Dilham, but the repeal of the Corn Laws in 1846 precipitated an agricultural recession. At Felbrigg a period of decline was accelerated in the disastrous reign of 'Mad Windham' and finally resulted in the sale of the much reduced estate to John Ketton in 1863. Ketton's son Robert neglected the estate after 1890, but much of this damage was made good by the Ketton-Cremers, who took over in 1924. In the 20th century there were no further acquisitions, and the estate is now one-fifth of its size in 1854. Four different farms are held by tenants.

The Park

The park today divides into three distinct parts. Deep woods lie to the north (known as the Great Wood) and the area of open parkland to the south of the house. The restored deer-park was present in the 16th century, but its origins were doubtless more ancient.

Until the 17th century, landowners relied largely on the management of existing indigenous woodland, and William Windham I was one of the first to usher in the age of plantations. His copy of the second edition of John Evelyn's *Sylva* of 1670 on practical arboriculture remains in the Library.

A little plan of 1691 shows an ambitious woodland layout to the north of the hall, covering much of the area which Windham described as 'sowne with severalle sorts of Corne'. The 30 per cent drop in corn prices in 1689, the year of Windham's death, could well have prompted this grand new planting by his widow Katherine, and what remains of it today is represented by the ragged old sweet chestnuts to the north of the house.

The Great Wood was progressively enlarged during the course of the next two centuries, and anyone who walks through it today will soon come across the series of three long sickle-shaped banks which represent its expanding northern boundary in the late 17th century, in 1777 under William Windham III, and in 1826. William Windham I planted conifers as well as deciduous trees.

The 18th century at Felbrigg is chiefly remarkable for the plantations of William Windham III, undertaken by Nathaniel Kent. Between 1770 and 1788 he made more than thirteen different new plantations, some of them no more than clumps, others extensive belts and woods. They included in 1778 the Marble Hill Clump, the Church Close Plantations and the Triangle Plantation, in 1779 the Church Circle, in the 1780s plantings west of Round Wood, the wood near the Mustard Pot, Sexton Wood and much else besides. This work was contemporary with Humphry Repton's employment as Windham's secretary, and he may have been involved in some way, even though he had yet to begin his career as a professional landscape designer. The park is certainly Reptonian in character, with its gracefully sculpted clumps and belts, and the ingeniously meandering approach from the Marble Hill to the south-east, which in the 18th century gave visitors the best possible impression of the scale and natural beauty of the park without taking them much out of their way.

The woods and the parkland were much neglected at the close of the 19th century and remained so until the Ketton-Cremers arrived in 1924. They planted very large numbers of trees, and at the end of the Second World War Ketton-Cremer celebrated the allied victory with a V-shaped plantation behind the house.

Since 1993 the Trust has made a series of Farm Stewardship agreements with its tenant farmers to put down to grass areas of the park that have for many years been in arable cultivation. Trees and hedges have been planted, and other conservation measures implemented. The main tenant now farms organically.

Felbrigg and its owners

The Felbriggs

The name Felbrigg is a relic of the Danish invasions: *Fiol-brygga* is ancient Scandinavian for a plank bridge. When the Norman invaders made their Domesday survey in 1086, the village was amongst the many possessions of the Bigod family. The earliest record of a family taking Felbrigg as its name comes from the late 11th century, when Ailward de Felbrigg and his kinsmen were joined by marriage to the Bigods. In the chancel of nearby St Margaret's church is a monumental brass which is unusual in depicting two successive lords of the manor and their wives. The first, Simon de Felbrigg, is thought to have died in 1351 and is shown with his wife Alice de Thorp. Next to them, in armour, is their son Roger and his wife Elizabeth. Roger was a soldier who fought in France in the 1350s and was one of the earliest of Felbrigg's many owners to travel abroad.

Felbrigg church, which Sir Simon Felbrigg probably rebuilt in the early 15th century

The brass was probably laid by Roger's famous son, Sir Simon Felbrigg, who had been born in about 1366 and was to follow in his father's footsteps, joining the service of John of Gaunt and fighting alongside him and other Norfolk knights in France and Spain. By 1394 he had found a place at the court of Richard II and was described as a 'king's knight'. A year later he was made royal standard bearer with an annual payment of £100. He was made a Knight of the Garter in 1397 and so entered the most exclusive of the orders of chivalry. His marriage to Margaret, daughter of Premyslaus, Duke of Teschen, and maid of honour to Richard II's first queen, Anne of Bohemia, showed the regard in which he was held by the royal household. The Lancastrian coup of 1399 spelt disaster for Sir Simon, who was deprived of his lucrative offices by the new king, Henry IV. His last ceremonial duty, the escorting of Richard's second queen, Isabel, into exile in 1400, was a melancholy assignment and although he retained his garter stall, he seems never to have attended Chapters under the new regime. The death of his first wife in 1416 was the occasion for the making of one of the most splendid of English monumental brasses for Felbrigg church. Studded with the heraldry of Richard II and Bohemia, it was at once a defiant declaration and wistful symbol of the departed glory. When Sir Simon Felbrigg died in December 1442 and was buried with his second wife in the choir of the Norwich Blackfriars' church, his will provided for masses to be said for the soul of 'Richard, lately king of England' and instructed that Felbrigg be sold.

The Wyndhams

One of Sir Simon Felbrigg's trustees obtained the reversion of the estate and sold it in about 1450 to John Wymondham (later contracted to Wyndham), who had held land near Wymondham in south Norfolk since 1436. Wyndham took up residence in the face of

Sir Simon Felbrigg (d. 1442) and his first wife Margaret (d. 1416); etching by J. S. Cotman of the tomb brass in Felbrigg church

Bedingfeld of Oxburgh, knighted by Henry VII for service at the Battle of Stoke in 1487. He became, however, an associate of Edmund de la Pole, Earl of Suffolk, who in 1501 conspired with the Emperor Maximilian to overthrow the King. Sir John, closely implicated, died on the scaffold on 6 May 1502 alongside Tyrrel, prime suspect for the murder in 1483 of the Princes in the Tower, the young heirs to the Yorkist claim to the throne.

In spite of this setback, John's son Thomas made a name for himself in the navy, fighting against the French and ultimately gaining a place in Henry VIII's Council. He acquired great wealth, and may have built the earliest surviving parts of Felbrigg Hall. Under the south front are considerable remains of an early Tudor house: archways, a door with rich linenfold panelling, and, projecting under the forecourt, a cellar with a four-centred brick barrel vault. He died in 1522 and his son Edmund further bolstered the estate during the 1530s by acquiring Beeston Priory at a knock-down price during the Dissolution of the Monasteries. As High Sheriff of Norfolk, Edmund organised the execution of the Ketts and their followers after the bloody suppression of their uprising in 1549.

With the inheritance of Edmund's son Roger in 1569, Felbrigg entered one of the most unhappy periods in its long history. The new squire set about the persecution of his neighbours and their connections with a zeal which, properly directed, might have consolidated his inheritance. He went to court at the least excuse, 'from stranded wrecks to straying horses and broken fences'. His activities so depleted the resources of the estate that he was compelled to mortgage much of it to his wealthy cousin Sir John Wyndham, who presided over the flourishing junior branch of the family at Orchard Wyndham in Somerset. When Roger died in 1599, his only significant contribution to the distinction of the Norfolk branch was the institution of the modern spelling of Windham, and the widespread odium which then attached to the name. It fell to his youngest brother Thomas to receive this mixed inheritance, and providence gave him less than a year in which to make something of it.

angry demonstrations by the villagers. In 1461, the year of Lady Felbrigg's death, Sir John Felbrigg (the head of another branch of the family) and a band of sympathisers appeared at the house in Wyndham's absence and dragged his wife out of her locked room by the hair. Wyndham declared that he would be back by Michaelmas or there would be 'five hundred heads broke therefor', but eventually Sir John Felbrigg accepted a cash settlement and withdrew. Wyndham's son, another John, who succeeded in 1475, was, like Sir Edmund

A new start

Thomas Windham began by renouncing everything that his brother had done and promised an immediate return to his father's more benign manorial customs. Moreover, as Roger had neglected to consult him, as an heir-at-law, over the mortgages to Sir John Wyndham, these were declared void. But Thomas made clear that, should he fail to marry and have children, then the reversion of the entire estate would pass to Sir John and with this important proviso:

Finally I do greatly desire that the said inheritance coming to my said cosin, the same might continually be inhabited, and the house of Felbrigg be dwelt upon, either by himself, or by some of his children of the name; so that the name might be continued with some countenance in this county, and in this lyneal succession, where the eldest house hath always remained.

As another Felbrigg winter settled in, Thomas Windham, having done more in a few months to enhance the family reputation than his brother had done in 30 years, died on 20 December 1599, leaving the hall in the occupation of his sister Jane Coningsby. She had kept house for him and was allowed to remain there until her death in 1608. For Sir John Wyndham it was a sensible and economic arrangement. After 1608 he had to run Felbrigg from Somerset, sending his servant John Blinman on arduous journeys across the country to draw up the accounts. One of Blinman's first jobs was to list the contents of the hall and the farm stock and to determine what should remain at Felbrigg; what should go to 'My Lord' at Orchard Wyndham; and what should be sent to 'Mr Thomas' in London. 'Mr Thomas', a London lawyer, was Sir John's third son and the fact that he was now able to draw on the resources of the central part of the estate indicated that he had been chosen to refound the Norfolk Windhams.

(Right) The south front, built by Sir John Wyndham and his son Thomas in 1621–4

Some of the best furnishings and plate were packed off to Orchard, including 'a Tester of a bed of Crimson velvet with vallance and curtains thereto belonging and curtains of Taffetie Sarsenett [silk taffeta]'. Basic furniture, 'chairs, stools and suchlike' stayed at Felbrigg. The richest of Mrs Coningsby's clothes went to Orchard; some remained, while others were divided among her maids. The splendid plate, which would have been displayed at feasts in the old great hall, was split between Sir John and Thomas, who got the spoons and a representative collection of grand pieces including a parcel gilt ewer and basin, a silver gilt goblet, a great silver bowl and the remainder of the plate.

In December 1620 Thomas married Elizabeth, daughter of Sir Rowland Lytton of Knebworth in Hertfordshire, and, in the expectation of founding a new dynasty at Felbrigg, he set about rebuilding the house with his father. The Chief Justice of the Common Pleas, Sir Henry Hobart, had assembled a considerable team of workmen for the rebuilding of Blickling Hall about eight miles south of Felbrigg in 1619. The exact repetition of certain devices and details leaves no real doubt that Hobart's architect, Robert Lyminge, or a close associate, was also responsible for the new Felbrigg.

Work was already quite advanced when the sparse Felbrigg building accounts commence in 1621. Some of the earliest entries are in the hand of Elizabeth Windham, who was to die after

giving birth to an heir in 1622. In February Matthews the bricklayer was paid for paving the cellars. Edward Stanyon the plasterer, whose splendid ceilings may be seen at Blickling, also received payment. It was quite usual at this period for the builder of a house to enter into separate agreements with numerous contractors, so we find mention of several other craftsmen: Stockdale the carpenter and 'his bargin for the stairs' of £33; Christopher the joiner, Linacre the glazier, and in 1624 Smith the mason, who was paid for the two stone lions which surmount the east and west gables, and no doubt made the other parapet figures. The house must have been nearly complete at this time.

Above the entrance are the coats of arms of Sir John Wyndham of Orchard Wyndham in Somerset, his wife Joan Portman, their son Thomas and his first wife Elizabeth Lytton. They celebrated the re-establishment of the family at Felbrigg by building the south front

There may have been more to the building than the south front we see today, as the accounts indicate that parts of the ancient house were retained. In February 1623 'the hard stone men' were paid 2s 6d 'For setting the harth pase [stone] in the ould great chamber', which must have been part of an existing structure and probably outside the present 1620s work.

The design of Jacobean Felbrigg was typical of its period. The ground plan with the central porch leading into a screens passage with the great hall to the west and the butteries, pantry and kitchen to the east finds more than one parallel in the plans of houses drawn by the Smythsons in the late 16th century. But it bears a particularly intimate resemblance to Crewe Hall in Cheshire, which was begun in 1615 by Sir Randulph Crewe, an ambitious lawyer who was to become Lord Chief Justice in 1625. He had Norfolk connections and would have been well known to Sir Henry Hobart and Thomas Windham, who were both also lawyers.

The significance of the house as a new start for the Windhams in Norfolk is proclaimed in its decoration. The coats of arms above the front door are those of Sir John Wyndham and of his son Thomas and their wives. The involvement of two generations is also implied

in the heraldic decoration at Blickling, but where Felbrigg differs from most houses of the period is in the prominence given to the great religious message of its first-floor parapet, 'gloria deo in excelsis'. It would certainly have appealed to the Jacobean taste for the witty 'device' to place 'Glory to God in the Highest' on the highest part of the building, but Thomas Windham was perhaps mindful of those powerful passages in Deuteronomy where the Law is given in the context of establishing a place in a new land: 'What man is there that hath built a new house, and hath not dedicated it?' (xx.5). Included among the misfortunes predicted for those who forget God in Chapter 28 is '… thou shalt build a house and not dwell therein; thou shalt plant a vineyard and not use the fruit thereof'. It was a very real prospect. Elizabeth Windham had already gone and soon Sir Henry Hobart was to die before he had a chance to enjoy Blickling, but Thomas Windham and his father both lived on for many years, and the branch which had been replanted in Norfolk flourished anew.

William (1647–89) and Katherine Windham (1652–1729)

With the coming of the Civil War in 1642, Thomas Windham became an active supporter of Parliament. As High Sheriff of Norfolk in 1639–40 it had been his task to collect the King's hated 'Ship Money' tax from the county. Most of Norfolk became solidly Parliamentarian and Thomas served on the Committee for the Eastern Association. His elder son John became a captain of horse. Whereas the few Royalist houses, for example Oxburgh, that found themselves behind enemy lines suffered some violence, for Felbrigg the war meant only anxiety and economic hardship.

Thomas Windham died on 1 March 1654, attended by Dr Thomas Browne, the author of *Religio Medici*, one of the most famous 17th-century confessions of faith. The eleven-year reign at Felbrigg of his son John was uneventful so far as the house and estate were concerned but was marked by personal tragedies. He buried three wives, produced no surviving heir and died in 1665, little more than a year after his fourth marriage. His half-brother William, who had been born to Thomas Windham's second wife, Elizabeth Mede, in 1647, came of age in 1668 and during the next 21 years was to leave an indelible mark on Felbrigg. In 1669 he married Katherine, daughter of Sir Joseph Ashe, a wealthy merchant of Twickenham in Middlesex who traded with the Low Countries. Katherine, who survived her husband by 40 years, became a most likeable matriarch and was the backbone of the family until her death in 1729.

William Windham ran the estate himself, recording all his doings in two vellum-covered ledgers. The second of these, stained a bright green with brass clasps, is among the most important records of estate management in England at this period. The prospect of major building operations was heralded in 1675, when he noted, 'I felled all the Timber used about my new building at Felbrigg'. Drawings for the extension of the house were prepared for Windham by the gentleman architect William Samwell in August 1674. The first ground plan proposed to double its size with three new fronts around a courtyard. The second, in February 1675, reduced the scheme by half to a new west wing and, on the north-east corner, a one-room-deep addition to the back of the main Jacobean pile. 'I persuaded Mr Samwell to draw this against his fancye', Windham notes on the second drawing, 'by reason I thought his first design too bigg & not convenient, which caused him to write . . . [and here in Samwell's own hand] "This ill fourmed Beare",' after which Windham resumes, 'I like this very well altering ye Closet & Staires.' Below his signature are the words 'built Anno: 75'. The handsome drawing of the west elevation by Samwell shows yet another phase in the design process. Whereas the first two had suggested a west façade which included and remodelled the west gable of the Jacobean house, the elevation drawing expresses the wing as a distinct unit, and implies the arresting contrast between old and new which the west front presents today.

William Samwell was a skilled practitioner of the new Restoration classicism, and his front at Felbrigg preserves better than any surviving example of his work his sophisticated grasp of detail and proportion. But Samwell died in the summer of 1676. Given that the exterior of the west wing was not finished until about 1686, it is unlikely that he saw more than the building of the north-eastern extension. This has a different string course from the west wing, and it is on this part of the second drawing that Windham's words 'built Anno: 75' are inscribed.

It may have been the master carpenter Skidmore who carried Samwell's plans forward in the 1680s. His assistant Thomas Vidler was to stay on until the next century and received extensive payments. Miles Skerry, variously described as bricklayer and mason, may have been responsible for the wonderful brickwork of the new wing, and there are also payments to a Michael Skerry. Especially interesting in view of the house Samwell built for Charles II at Newmarket is the note in August 1683 that a 'Newmarket man' was paid 'to set the clamp of 100,000 bricks'. These were probably special bricks for the facing of the wing. In 1685

William Windham I (1647–89), who built the west front; by Sir Peter Lely (Dining Room)

Windham ordered the felling of more timber 'used about my building'. Sir Jacob Astley of Melton Constable, whose great new house was rising at the same time, provided some lead for Felbrigg.

By 1686, the date on one of the west front rainwater heads, the main structure was complete. On the ground floor the new wing provided a Great Staircase, a new Great Parlour for dining, and beyond it a smaller withdrawing room. On the first floor were two large rooms and a pair of closets. There was much fitting-out to do. The marvellous plaster ceiling of the Great Parlour (now the Drawing Room) is dated 1687, and is clearly by the plasterer who made the contemporary ceilings at Melton Constable – probably Edward Goudge, one of the greatest craftsmen of the period. In May 1688 there is an early payment to Cornwell the painter, and Goodwife Hilton was sent in to clean the building. In April the following year panels for the Great Parlour were supplied by Knowles the joiner from Holt, who was paid that September for laying floors in 'the New Building'. In May Caston the local carpenter (possibly a member of the Cawston family who were to work as estate carpenters until the late 19th century) was paid

for framing the cellar windows on the garden side and for laying the floor of the Great Stairs. The final touches were being made to the Great Parlour in October when 1s was paid for 'a seale skin to Rub the wainscot', 2s 'for lyne to hang the picktures in the new parlour'. Cornwell varnished the panels from a scaffold made by Caston.

The west wing caused a revolution in the local architecture. Aylsham Old Hall was being built simultaneously and not far away by another branch of the family and exhibits many identical details, as do numerous houses and imposing barns in Aylsham, Coltishall and other parts of the Bure valley until the mid-18th century. But not everyone was so impressed by the amenities of the 'New Appartment'. Roger North, the virtuoso who lived at Rougham in Norfolk, while acknowledging the general acclaim, was particularly critical of the staircase which the local carpenters had built in what is now the Dining Room to a plan different from the one envisaged by Samwell. North wrote of it: 'however pompous and costly in the frame and finishing, doth not stupifie the sense, so as to make the pains of mounting three or four stretching flights insensible.'

Samwell's elevation drawing for the west front, c.1675

The last payments for the exterior of the new wing are recorded by Katherine Windham as executrix of her husband's will, for, as she wrote in her first little notebook, 'My Dear Dear Husband left me the 9th June 1689 having made me Hapy 20 years.' William Windham's life at Felbrigg had been a reasonably tranquil one, after some initial quarrels with importunate relations, and in spite of the persistent entreaties of Sir John Hobart of Blickling, he had managed to avoid much involvement in politics: 'I confess I take soe much delight in my Nursery and Garden that I don't envye the Knight the honour of being in the house', he had written in 1679.

Katherine Windham presided over Felbrigg and its family during the minority of her eldest son, Ashe, who had been given her maiden name. He was now eighteen and, after Eton, was completing his education at its sister foundation, King's College, Cambridge. Katherine Windham's love for Felbrigg and her children shines out of the numerous letters and accounts that record her life. She had been a girl of seventeen when she came to Felbrigg, and the earliest entries in her notebook, some of them in French, record fashionable clothes and trimmings, caged birds and a book on how to

Katherine Windham (1652–1729), who ran the Felbrigg estate after her husband's death; by Sir Peter Lely and Studio (Dining Room)

care for them, perfume, money lost and won at cards, gifts to the poor and books. Most of the latter were devotional, but a significant number were medical and herbal, and later she was relied upon by the family for herbal remedies.

There was much to occupy her bereavement. Her management of the estate and of the family finances is recorded in her *Fair Accounts since Midsummer 1689*. The family vault was repaired and a monument commemorating her husband ordered for the church from Grinling Gibbons. In 1687–8 she hung her drawing room with crimson and green damask with green and white fringing for £64. A large inlaid table and hanging looking-glass with a pair of candlestands were £18. She bought ten elbow chairs for £6 15s from Thomas Arne (a Covent Garden upholsterer and the father of the composer), had them japanned for £2 15s, upholstered for £4 4s, and everyday case covers made for £3. Eight silver sconces were £42, and for the fireplace she bought silver andirons, which, with matching dogs, shovel and tongs, came to £44.

Katherine Windham's *Book of Cookery and Housekeeping*, begun in 1707, is a fascinating record of a wealthy family's diet at the period. 'Artificial Sturgion', made from a whole boiled calf's head from which the bones are removed, sounds unappetising but there are many recipes that would be popular today. Some are named after family and friends: 'Lord Townshend's Puding', 'my son's Rice Puding', 'a very good Carroway Cake My Sister Townshend' and so on. There are remedies for getting flies out of rooms, and the section 'Concerning Buggs' recommends smearing the bedding with broken-up cucumbers or covering one's face and neck with lemon juice and wormwood.

Ashe Windham (1673–1749)

In 1692 Patrick St Clair was appointed as Ashe's tutor and in 1693, the year before the new squire came of age, the two of them set off on the Grand Tour. On their return in 1696 St Clair was presented to the living of Aylmerton. In 1694 we find the first recorded payment towards building the Orangery, which was one of the major undertakings of Ashe's early years. In 1697 the young orange trees were bought for £21.

'I design to find sashes workmanship shutters doors pavement for the orenge house', Katherine wrote in one of her typically chatty letters of February 1705, 'and you to find Bricke, lime, Timber, Tile & Cariage but all the money must be deducted out of what you owe me, which is at least 350, for I cant supply my children on your account & find money for everything. Wish I could & it should be at your service.' In the same letter she makes clear that there was still work to do in the west wing and suggests that Ashe 'may let alone the Glasse & Harths & Chairs till another time for with the bed curtains & Ha[n]gings the romes may be used this year the smell of the paint will not be quickly out'; an aside probably connected with a small group of drawings for two of the first-floor rooms (the present Rose and Red Bedrooms) in the west wing, made to calculate the size of hangings and to indicate different treatments for fireplaces and chimney-glasses. In November 1704 Elden the carpenter had been paid for work about the new building. Whereas the windows of the Great Parlour had iron bars and must, therefore, have been of the old mullion-and-transom type with leaded lights, as shown in Samwell's drawing, these two rooms are shown with sashes, and this novel type of window was to be the most prominent feature of the new Orangery.

The drawings for the Orangery are unsigned, but Ashe may have been its

architect. A plain but well-proportioned building, it is a perfect neighbour for the west wing, and might have been more decorative had Katherine Windham not been in charge of operations in Ashe's absence, for the letter quoted above includes the remark, 'We country folks are too dull to understand what you mean by ornaments.'

One of the notable features of the estate accounts during the first decade of the 18th century is the crescendo of activity in the brick-works. William Barrett received advance payment in December 1702 for 100,000 bricks to be made in the coming year. In November 1703 200,000 more were ordered and the same amount in October 1704. This intense period of activity during which the kiln was fed with bracken, rushes, brushwood and whatever happened to be harvested at the time, subsided towards the end of the decade. The Orangery was one cause and so was the continuing repair of the park wall, and there was work on other estate buildings. But Ashe had also taken on the

(Right) Ashe Windham (1673–1749), who built the Orangery; by Sir Godfrey Kneller (Dining Room)

task of completely rebuilding the domestic offices at the house around a spacious courtyard and remodelling the garden.

Annotated drawings in Ashe's hand show how deeply involved he was in surveying the site of the new service buildings on the west side of the house and overcoming the problems of differential levels which it presented. The west side of the new courtyard contained servants' hall, kitchen, bake-house and meat room. The north range accommodated a deer-house or dairy, the wash-house, malt-house and brew-house, and a new granary ran at right-angles on the east side. The south side was formed by a narrow building which contained scullery, pastry room, dry larder, the cook's chamber and, at the far end, the keeper's chamber. Most of these buildings survive, and were probably complete by 1711, when a joiner was paid for some of the wash-house furniture, but the south range was to be replaced by Ashe's son in the 1750s and the north and west ranges were substantially remodelled thereafter. Only the granary perfectly preserves its original character and is one of the most pleasing buildings on the estate.

Money was not a problem for Ashe Windham, whose father's various loans and investments produced a healthy income. These new buildings of course implied a large household. His liveried servants wore blue coats with red waistcoats and included Dutch and Italian footmen. The park keeper was allowed the distinction of a 'coat and waistcoat of Green Cloth and breeches of green shagg'. Between 1695 and 1709 Ashe spent nearly £243 on his own clothes and £187 on livery. He was in every respect an eligible young man, and the decade which saw so much building activity at Felbrigg witnessed much else in the life of the family. In 1704 his younger brother, William, lost his leg at the battle of Blenheim and wrote home to his mother about it with extraordinary courage and cheerfulness. Ashe was elected to Parliament in 1708, but gave up the seat two years later. Early in 1708 he met the love of his life in Hester Buckworth and showered her with over £285 worth of jewels, much to his mother's annoyance. In anticipation of their

Hester Buckworth, Ashe Windham's fiancée, who died of smallpox in 1708, before they could marry; studio of Sir Godfrey Kneller (Stair Hall)

marriage, Katherine decided to decamp to a house of her own at Braxted in Essex, but Hester Buckworth died of smallpox before the year was out. The large portrait of her, which hangs above the door to the Dining Room in the Stair Hall, must have acquired added poignancy as the years went by, especially when Ashe's relationship with the attractive but neurotic Elizabeth Dobyns – married on the rebound in 1709 with another £472 worth of jewels – gradually went sour. Their only child, William, was born in 1717, and three years later the squire and his wife finally separated. The 1720s were difficult years in which the family lost huge sums in the collapse of the South Sea Bubble and in which Ashe contracted a mysterious and chronic illness that was to keep him away from Felbrigg for long periods.

When Katherine Windham died in 1729 at the age of 78, Ashe's own generation was already falling away. His brother James had died at sea near Honduras in 1724. Colonel William Windham died in 1730 and Ashe's estranged wife Elizabeth followed in 1736. Many hopes must have been pinned on the next generation, represented by the solitary figure of Ashe's son William.

William Windham II (1717–61)

William Windham II was destined by upbringing and temperament to form as strong a bond with Felbrigg as any of its previous inhabitants. He was saved from the rigours of boarding school and did not attend any university. Patrick St Clair remained at Felbrigg to instruct him, and in 1723 Benjamin Stillingfleet was appointed his personal tutor. This eccentric and agreeable scholar, the grandson of the Bishop of Worcester, was to publish works on mathematics, music, society and natural history. The blue worsted stockings which he wore at the literary soirées held by Mrs Vesey became a shorthand for intellectual womankind. If one looks at the books which his pupil bought for the library at Felbrigg, it is not difficult to see how influential Stillingfleet had been in forming the very catholic tastes of the new squire.

In 1738 tutor and pupil set out on a tour of the Continent from which they were not to

William Windham II (1717–61), who created the Cabinet; pastel painted by Barthélémy du Pan, probably in Geneva, where Windham was living from 1738 to 1742

Richard Aldworth, a fellow member of the Common Room, on William Windham II:

'Windham, tall, thin, and narrow-chested, would vie with Price in every feat of strength and agility, and so far he succeeded that he was known through London by the name of Boxing Windham; whilst few knew his quiet friend Mr Price could box at all. Fewer yet could divine that Mr Windham would have excelled in almost every pursuit but those he was seen to follow; that he possessed Greek, Latin, Spanish, and French, to a high degree; and knew something of Dutch and German. This was, however, the fact; and from those various sources, his amazing parts, equally quick and retentive, had drawn and amassed treasures of science and amusement, which was the more striking from his apparent dissipation: he was besides a mathematician, mechanic and draughtsman; could and did build vessels, and navigate them himself; in short, he was every thing.'

return until 1742. They went first to Geneva and then spent some months in Rome. But by the winter of 1739–40 they were back in Geneva. Here, with a group of young English friends and their tutors, Windham formed a club known as 'the Common Room'. Their light-hearted but historic expedition in June 1741 to the Mer de Glace is still commemorated by a plaque on the edge of the glacier. In the plays which they put on for their own amusement Stillingfleet wrote the music and was in charge of the stage machinery.

In 1740 Windham was betrothed to Elisabeth de Chapeaurouge, the daughter of the First Syndic of Geneva, but his image of her was to fade rapidly on his return to England, although it was not until 1751 that he finally extricated himself from this commitment, at some considerable expense. Windham and Stillingfleet began their return journey via the Low Countries in July 1742. In the seven years before his father's death, William was to pursue

During his Grand Tour William Windham II acquired a fine collection of architectural books, which are still in the Library

his own existence away from Felbrigg, taking a house in London with his friend Robert Price of Foxley and renting country retreats in Essex and Warwickshire. He developed a long-lasting friendship with David Garrick which is commemorated in a charming double portrait by Francis Hayman that Garrick commissioned in about 1745.

In the early 1740s Hayman had collaborated with the architect James Paine on a number of jobs in the north of England, and it was probably through this connection that Windham came to employ Paine at Felbrigg. Work had begun by 1749, and from then on we can follow its progress through Windham's account books and in the numerous friendly and animated letters of instruction which he sent to his agent Robert Frary.

The first task for Paine was the construction of a new service wing to take the place of the narrow southern service range put up by Ashe, as well as some alterations to the north range. This new wing was important to Windham not just because it allowed for the creation of a new servants' hall, steward's room and audit room

The great explosion

Windham has a passion for fireworks, but the great explosion of 27 December 1755 probably brought Windham's interest in pyrotechnics to a premature end. It entirely destroyed his firework shop, whose roof was blown over the top of the granary and was later found blazing in the coalyard. Windows were smashed throughout the service yard, and everyone considerably shaken up.

but because it also incorporated the workshops where he could follow the many practical interests hinted at by Richard Aldworth, which included wood-turning and bookbinding (see p. 29).

The new service wing also provided useful storage space in the early 1750s, when the state rooms were in turmoil. The wing's foundations had been dug by July 1749 and on 13 August John Baxter was paid for carting 20,000 bricks to the 'Offices'. The builder was Francis Pank and in November of the same year he was paid for making floors and ceilings. In November rubbish was being cleared out of the new building and just before Christmas a neighbour, Bozoon Brigge, who must have had pale brick earth not available at Felbrigg, was paid for the white paving bricks of the workshop floors. It is in the construction of these attractive service rooms that we first encounter the joiner George Church, who was to make nearly all the fitted woodwork and some of the movable furniture during the five years of Windham's extensive remodelling.

The servants' wing was being furnished in January 1751 and by now much progress had been made in the house. The 1680s west wing was deepened on its east side by an extension that housed ground- and first-floor passages (the present Stone and West Corridors), bringing greater privacy to rooms which had previously opened into one another. At the north end a two-storey polygonal bay extended what had been the Drawing Room and the two little rooms above it.

The old Drawing Room with its new bay window was now to be known as the Cabinet, and the accounts sometimes refer to it as the 'best room'. Although tackled first, the Cabinet was clearly conceived as the climax of a sequence of ground-floor rooms. The Great Parlour was also remodelled with handsome new joinery, and the Eating Room (now the Dining Room) took the place of the 1680s stair-case, whose successor rose immediately to the east. On the first floor the removal of the old stairs and the introduction of the bay made possible a suite of two bedrooms with spacious and richly appointed dressing rooms, and with the luxury of a decent corridor. This left a little gap at the south end and here Windham contrived his own modest dressing room (now known as the Grey Dressing Room). It did not need to be large because it had a private door into the great new Library which took up nearly half of the south front and which communicated with the bedroom (now the Book Room) which he shared with his wife.

Sarah Lukin (née Hicks) was the widow of Robert Lukin of Dunmow in Essex, by whom she had had three children. When, at the age of 40, Sarah married Windham in February 1750, the two had been living together for several years and she was already heavily pregnant with his child. In May she gave birth to a son, another William and, like his father, an only child. It was after this that Windham began the complex and expensive negotiations that would release him from his obligations to Elizabeth de Chapeaurouge in Geneva.

The work at Felbrigg was subject to the usual delays, and Windham became irate. On 3 March 1752 he wrote:

I have just received a letter from Paine with a drawing of the staircase which I send you. He says he has had an inflammation of his eyes which has prevented his finishing the drawings &c humbug.

I have wrote to Mr Field to speak to him roundly & told him we would send him heads of accusations from Felbrigg. I think the staircase too much ornamented according to that draught.

Especially stressful was the business of co-ordinating the London craftsmen to produce their goods in time to be shipped by Mr Worsted to Felbrigg in June:

Worsted is come and I have been in the cursedest passion imaginable with all the workmen about the things. Carter who was to have done the chimney-piece sent me word that he could not get the chimney done before the end of next month upon which I sent to stop all his doings & sure I would not have the chimney at all ... as for Biggs I have stopped all his work & will send you the drawings for to have the chimney for the eating parlour to be done by our own workmen. Bladwell will have everything ready by Thursday & we will endeavour to keep Worsted till the medals are ready and will be sent down. The pictures are now preparing and will be ready very soon....

Bladwell the upholsterer, of Bow Street, Covent Garden, who also provided furniture for Uppark in Sussex and Holkham in Norfolk, proved to be the most reliable of the London men and was paid very large sums for furniture of superb quality, including some lovely Rococo looking-glasses in the Cabinet. Mirror glass was still extraordinarily expensive, and Windham obtained measured drawings of all the 17th-century mirrors in the house so that the new frames would fit their plates. The gilded picture frames which do so much to enliven the rooms were made by either René

Duffour in Soho or Thomas Quintin, who worked on site at Felbrigg. Quintin did the ornate architectural carving that was beyond Church, whose ingenuity was sometimes a source of annoyance for Windham. 'I am very glad', he wrote in April 1753, 'that Church makes so many pockets in my dressing room for I think there cannot be too many but I desire no fine conundrums of killing the devil and making places that in hard using will neither open nor shut.'

In spite of their disagreements, Paine and Windham created a marvellous synthesis of architecture, decoration and furnishing cleverly attuned to the historic character of the house. Some owners would have wanted to modernise the south front and in so doing reduce the discord between it and the west wing. But not Windham, who responded warmly to its ancient

The Tomb of Cecilia Metella; by Pietro Bianchi. One of William Windham II's Grand Tour commissions for the Cabinet

charm in his treatment of its rooms. The Great Hall became sober, simplified neo-Tudor with plaster busts on brackets, and the Gothic book-cases of the new Library above it conveyed the same message of continuity with the ancient work. They housed a collection swelled by Windham's purchases in Italy, Geneva and the Low Countries, some of them bound by their owner. The Stair Hall was also decorated with busts, as was the new Eating Room, which was hung with portraits of the previous two generations who had first built and furnished the west wing.

The delicately tinted plaster walls of the Great Hall, Stair Hall and Eating Room were a deliberate contrast with the sumptuous colour and gilding in the Great Parlour (now Drawing Room) and Cabinet beyond. Here, although the Caroline plasterwork was retained and embellished, Knowles's old panelling was removed to provide clear fields which could be hung with the trophies of Windham's Grand Tour. The newly papered walls of the Great Parlour were given over to Old Masters and in particular splendid marine pictures by the Van de Veldes and Samuel Scott. Those of the Cabinet, hung with damask, were dominated by the landscapes of Giovanni Battista Busiri: large oils of Tivoli, Frascati and Città Castellana, and little gouaches of monuments in the Roman countryside from which the sunshine still glows warmly after more than two centuries. The work went on until January 1755, when Church fitted out the Library.

Windham seems to have had no ambition other than to lead a full and active life and to make enjoyable use of his many gifts. He was never called upon to do otherwise, except when war came in 1756 and he became involved in the local militia at the instigation of his Norfolk friend and distant relative, the Hon. George Townshend. There were no readily available instructions for the training of the new militias so Windham gave much time to the production of *A Plan of Discipline, composed for the use of the Militia of the County of Norfolk* before its publication in 1759. He died of consumption in October 1761, leaving a brilliant son who had inherited many of his gifts.

William Windham III (1750–1810)

The young William Windham was in his fourth year at Eton when his father died. 'Fighting Windham', as he was known to his fellows, could look after himself. He had been placed under the care of the Lower Master, his father's old friend Thomas Dampier, who in 1766 was forced to send him home for his prominent part in the school rebellion against the unpopular new headmaster, Dr Foster. At Oxford his self-discipline and capacity for work were legendary; he enjoyed and retained throughout his life a remarkable facility in mathematics as well as a wide and profound knowledge of classics. But his emotional life was curiously unsatisfactory.

Having made the acquaintance of the attractive Juliana Forrest and her equally alluring daughters, on coming down from Oxford in 1770, he fell for the eldest, Bridget, who was already married to John Byng, the solitary traveller of the Torrington Diaries, and for the next few years settled into a debilitating regime of frustrated devotion. It was not until 1775

William Windham III (1750–1810) delivering his first important political speech, in Norwich in 1778. This sketch is by his aide, Humphry Repton, later to become famous as a landscape gardener

that he began to develop an interest in her sister Cecilia, whose unrequited feelings for Windham's closest friend, George James Cholmondeley, were well known. Diaries record his uneasy visits to Felbrigg in these years, when he would stalk the empty rooms vainly trying to focus on some worthwhile activity. The academic projects which he set himself were never sufficient to retain his interest, and it was only the cut and thrust of national politics that were to inspire his great powers of concentration and the eloquence for which he was to have few rivals.

His political début was a memorable speech against the continuation of the American War, delivered at a public meeting in Norwich in 1778. His first public post, in 1783 as Chief Secretary to the Lord Lieutenant of Ireland and Leader of the Irish House of Commons, was cut short in a matter of months by illness. In 1784 he gained a seat in Parliament as the member for Norwich, with the future landscape gardener Humphry Repton, who had been his secretary in Ireland, as his election manager. Windham did not distinguish himself until 1788, when he helped mastermind the impeachment of Warren Hastings.

As a disciple of Edmund Burke, he had a particular horror of the French Revolution and when, in 1793, France declared war, Windham was a powerful advocate of a sustained and effective response. His group formed a coalition with Pitt's government in 1794 and Windham began a seven-year appointment as Secretary at War. When Pitt resigned because of the King's obstruction of Catholic Emancipation in the negotiations for the Act of Union in 1801, Windham followed him into opposition and attacked the new Addington administration over the flimsy peace which it made with Bonaparte at Amiens the same year. Britain was provoked into a fresh declaration of war in 1803 and Addington was soon swept from office. Pitt was back, but because he acceded to the King's exclusion of Fox from the government, Windham and his group declared their opposition to Pitt. Somewhat unfairly, this behaviour earned him the nickname 'Weathercock Windham', but his dissatisfaction with Pitt was given unfortunate expression when, after the Prime Minister's premature death in 1806, Windham argued doggedly in Parliament against a public funeral and a monument in Westminster Abbey. He gained responsibility for the army again in the short-lived 'Ministry of all the Talents', headed by Grenville, and as Secretary for War and the Colonies he made enduring and valuable reforms in army pay and conditions, but did little of value in the field of strategy.

In 1775 Windham had put Felbrigg under the care of Nathaniel Kent, who already had a reputation as an agent and agricultural improver, and during Kent's period much planting as well as the enclosure of common land took place. That the great politician made only a slight impression on the house is explained partly by his father's extensive remodelling and partly by his own inscrutable personal life. He married Cecilia Forrest as late as 1798 when they were both in their late forties and there was no prospect of a young family demanding changes or successors to enjoy them. The inventories which he conscientiously drew up on his coming of age in 1771 are an invaluable record of his father's 18th-century interiors. Between 1773 and 1777 he made a few small changes of his own and in 1788–9 the architect Robert Furze Brettingham was commissioned to make alterations. The closing-up of the west window of the Great Hall, the replacement of the Cabinet fireplace, the creation of a new butler's pantry and the addition of waterclosets are all documented, as is the fact that Windham's passion for learning required that the west window of the Library be sacrificed to new bookpresses. Light levels in the Library were further reduced by Brettingham's coloured glass in Gothic framing. His old friend Repton returned in 1806 to replace Paine's staircase lantern, and Brettingham's scheme for the new Morning Room, which finally replaced

William Windham III in his fifties; by John Jackson after Sir Thomas Lawrence (Drawing Room)

the old kitchen at the east end of the south front, was carried out in 1809.

In 1784 Windham had attended the bedside of his friend Samuel Johnson during the sage's final illness. The kindness and consideration he showed to Johnson then were examples of the unswerving loyalty which he could give to his true friends. The Library still contains some of Johnson's books, which were given during the old man's last days as keepsakes in recognition of Windham's devotion to learning. These two facets of Windham's character, and the physical courage learnt in his youth, were also displayed in the incident which led to his death on 4 June 1810. A painful malignancy on his hip, which required an agonising and fatal operation, was the result of an injury which he sustained while courageously saving the library of his friend Frederick North from a blazing house.

Admiral William Lukin Windham (1768–1833)

Windham had first thought of leaving Felbrigg to one of his close circle of friends but in the end settled it upon William, the eldest son of his half-brother George Lukin, who had been rector of Felbrigg and was now Dean of Wells. A distinguished sailor, whose life before the mast began in 1781 at the age of thirteen, William Lukin was to make his reputation in 1806 as the captain of the *Mars*, which, in an action off Rochefort, helped to capture four French troop ships. In the following year the *Mars* took part in the bombardment of Copenhagen. Lukin became a Vice-Admiral before he left the navy in 1814. The widowed Cecilia Windham, who now spent much of her time away from Norfolk, had a life-interest in Felbrigg, which meant that he could not enter into his inheritance until her death. So the Admiral bided his time with visibly increasing impatience in Felbrigg Parsonage, the boyhood home where he had been able to live since the removal of the rector to Metton.

With Cecilia Windham's passing in 1824, Lukin was now required to assume the name and arms of Windham as a surrogate heir. The house was woken from its fourteen years of slumber by a swift and sudden campaign of alterations by W. J. Donthorn, a local architect who at his best could produce work of great originality and power. Donthorn remodelled

William Lukin (1768–1833), who inherited Felbrigg from his uncle in 1824 (Morning Room)

Paine's service arcade as a passage with Gothic windows and pavilions at either end. The stable block rose to the east in castellated neo-Tudor and the whole of this significantly extended south front was given a coat of lime render, lined out to look like masonry. This work was completed with great expedition and perhaps too much economy in 1825. In 1831 the

The stable block was rebuilt by Admiral Lukin Windham in neo-Tudor style

Admiral remedied the main deficiency of the Dining Room by building what is now known as the Bird Corridor along the back of the south block to improve communication with the Kitchen.

The interior of the house was much enriched during these years. The family brought back sea pictures by Abraham Storck and Bakhuysen from their prolonged visit to Belgium in 1820–1. The elegant 18th-century rooms with their mahogany and walnut furniture were now augmented with new pieces: a billiard-table for the Great Hall, a new gilt and damask suite for the Great Parlour (which now became the Drawing Room) and some handsome four-posters for the bedrooms. The Regency taste for inlaid furniture expressed itself in some ingenious tables of rosewood and mahogany decorated with brass, and in the acquisition of French Boulle writing-tables and pedestals, the best of which is the splendid late 17th-century *bureau Mazarin* now in the Drawing Room. All these pieces are recorded in the inventory taken at the Admiral's death in 1833.

William Howe Windham (1802–54), who did much to modernise the estate (Morning Room)

William Howe Windham (1802–54)

His eldest son, William Howe Windham, had been born in 1802. He was away on the Grand Tour in 1824–5 and returned to a house strikingly transformed. He was to become a model improving landlord who, under the inspiration of Coke of Holkham, invested heavily in the farms, renewing their buildings, and punctiliously recording their construction with date stones in the gables (his alterations to the hall were recorded in the same way). He rose to county prominence as a Whig member for Norfolk in 1832, but lost his seat in 1837. It was perhaps with a politician's eye to self-advertisement that he put up two new pairs of lodges in the early 1840s, the grandest of which were built facing Cromer, by then a very fashionable resort, from which genteel tourists would make a bee-line for the hall. He also spent considerable sums on Felbrigg's most public room, the Great Hall. William Windham II's stripped Gothic interior with its little plaster busts, already substantially

remodelled by William Windham III, gave place to an early Victorian scheme with gargantuan neo-Jacobean details in which marble busts of past and present Whig heroes stood on plinths.

The windows were filled with stained glass both new and ancient, and in the new heraldic panels which decorated the reopened west window the squire celebrated his marriage, in 1835, to the daughter of the 1st Marquess of Bristol, Lady Sophia Hervey, whose family home, Ickworth in Suffolk, is now also in the care of the National Trust. The male members of Lady Sophia's family had a reputation for a certain eccentricity in looks and behaviour that stretched back to the early 18th century. She herself was highly strung, and her new husband's habit of shouting, whistling and singing to himself while alone in the Drawing Room was later remarked upon by the servants. So it was not perhaps entirely surprising that their son, who was born in 1840, turned into something of an oddity.

'Mad Windham' (1840–66)

William Frederick, who acquired the nickname 'Mad Windham' in the merciless climate of Victorian Eton, certainly had learning disabilities, and was further hampered by his upbringing. His passion for uniform was encouraged in early childhood when his parents gave him a little suit of the blue and red livery which the Felbrigg servants had worn since Ashe Windham's day. He was allowed to wait at table and spent his time in the Servants' Hall. As he grew up he became interested in trains and, having acquired a guard's uniform, could be found on the platforms of local stations causing chaos with unauthorised whistle blasts. His father died in 1854 and in due course Lady Sophia found consolation in the arms of Signor Giubilei, an Italian opera singer whom she had met in Torquay on an extended tour of watering places. Her son's education was neglected and

William Frederick Windham (1840–66). 'Mad Windham'

in the absence of parental affection his eccentricities became more pronounced.

This innocent came of age in 1861 and made his way to London where he dressed up as a policeman and patrolled the Haymarket, rounding up the dubious women who poured out of the pubs at closing time and urging the regular force to accompany them to the station. In the same year, on a visit to Ascot, he fell into the clutches of Agnes Willoughby, a glamorous kept woman whose protector, the timber contractor and notorious pimp 'Mahogany' Roberts, was soon to take an unhealthy interest in the Felbrigg woods. Agnes was a striking figure who sported a scarlet riding mantle at meetings of the Royal Buckhounds and was perpetually surrounded by crowds of admiring officers. Her blond hair and china doll complexion captivated Windham, as did the epithet 'pretty horsebreaker' which she and her kind attracted.

It was a perilous moment for Felbrigg and desperate measures were required when Windham assented to a generous marriage settlement which guaranteed an income for Agnes. His uncle, General Charles Windham, the bearded Crimean War hero of the assault on the Redan in 1855, found himself in an extremely awkward position. He wanted to protect the estate and its family from impending ruin but was compromised by his sons' interest as heirs. His petition for *De Lunatico Inquirendo*, to establish that his nephew was barred from entering into any marriage settlement, led to a notorious inquiry which made a marvellous spectacle for the press. The case was eventually found in his nephew's favour, and Windham was declared sane.

The marriage was predictably short-lived and Agnes soon fled from a husband she had always found distasteful to an old flame (coincidentally another Italian singer), returning only for two brief reconciliations, one of which she used to obtain the reversion of the Hanworth estate for the child with whom she was now pregnant. Windham's debts were completely out of control. The estate passed into the hands of his banker and was bought in 1863 by a Norwich merchant, John Ketton, who had made a fortune from oil-cake and cattle feed in the 1830s and '40s and altered his name from Kitton in 1853. 'Windham is gone to the dogs. Felbrigg has gone to the Kittens,' as the Rev. B.J. Armstrong recorded in his diary for January 1864.

Before his death in 1866 Windham remained a conspicuous figure in north Norfolk. He bought a mail van, had it painted scarlet, with the Windham arms, and drove it daily into Norwich for his letters. Then he became the owner and driver of a coach which travelled established routes, pinching the customers of other companies and giving them free trips until, after he had lost everything, he concluded with a spell as an increasingly erratic and dangerous driver of the express coach between Cromer and Norwich.

The Kettons and the Cremers

The Kettons made surprisingly little impact on Felbrigg. They moved in during March 1863 and lived happily in the old house with all its contents and memories for many years, and today there is almost no sign of them. John Ketton, who became rather cantankerous in later years, disinherited his elder son, and the estate passed to the younger brother Robert on his death in 1872. Robert Ketton's two youngest sisters, Marion and Gertrude, kept house for him. There are photographs of the Ketton girls sitting about in the rooms, playing billiards and enacting ghostly apparitions with clever double exposures. When first one sister and then the other died prematurely in the 1890s, Robert Ketton was devastated, and relapsed into a reclusive lifestyle in which the house and estate fell into decay. The few repairs that were done were met from the sale of

assets, and in 1918 and 1919 Ketton put some of the treasures of the house on the market, including Bladwell's splendid chairs and sofas from the Cabinet, some of the most important books from the Library and much of the porcelain.

Within five years he gave up and made over Felbrigg to his nephew, Wyndham Cremer, whose grandmother had been a Cromer Wyndham, descended from the younger brother of the builder of the house. Like Lukin, he was now required, as a condition of inheritance, to add another name to his own and so become Wyndham Ketton-Cremer. He had married Emily Bayly in 1905 and had only recently moved, in 1920, to Beeston Hall, north-west of Felbrigg. The Cremers had two sons, of whom the elder, Robert Wyndham Ketton-Cremer, was destined to become the last and most learned squire of Felbrigg.

The Cremers gave up an altogether manageable and agreeable house at Beeston and it says much for their sense of duty that they were prepared to take on the challenge of Felbrigg. The sale of some farms and of a few further contents including furniture and an important picture by Van Goyen, enabled the most formidable repairs to be tackled at the house and at the church, which was now virtually a ruin.

(Right) The Ketton sisters playing billiards in the Great Hall in the 1870s

The last squire of Felbrigg

Shortly after his father inherited the estate in 1924, Robert Wyndham Ketton-Cremer went up to Balliol. Here he suffered an attack of the rheumatic fever which had already plagued him at Harrow. His mother nursed him back to health, but he was left with a weak heart and with limited use of his right hand, and in later life he was rendered susceptible to a series of increasingly serious illnesses. These problems are made light of in Ketton-Cremer's account of the later history of Felbrigg in a characteristically stoical manner. He wrote little about himself in *Felbrigg: The Story of a House*, but a powerful sense of the man comes across in the writing. His real interest was in people and in what happened to them. He treated them with humanity and understanding in his daily dealings as in his fine books. His biographies of Horace Walpole (1940) and Thomas Gray (1955) are highly regarded and he gave up a project to write the life of Matthew Prior in order to tackle Felbrigg. He soaked himself in the culture and particularly the literature of the 18th century.

Respect for established institutions was reflected in old-fashioned Conservative politics, and a wariness of radicalism is plainly evident in his writing. He played, as his predecessors had done, a full part in the life of his county. As High Sheriff of Norfolk in 1951–2 he was required to witness two hangings, and as a JP he administered justice. His thorough knowledge of Norfolk churches made him an ideal chairman of the Norwich Diocesan Advisory Committee, and he was actively involved in the founding of the University of East Anglia, which conferred an honorary D. Litt on him in 1969, and to which he bequeathed his working library of books on Norfolk history.

(Right) Robert Wyndham Ketton-Cremer (1906–69), the last squire of Felbrigg; by Allan Gwynne-Jones (Great Hall)

His quiet demeanour could sometimes give way to anger. The explosion when a guest inconvenienced his staff by coming down late for dinner is recounted by Sir Brinsley Ford, and others wince at the memory of his wrath when he discovered someone smoking a cigarette in Felbrigg church. Devout Christianity was central to him and this, combined with a sense of duty inculcated by his parents, gave him a formidable strength of character. As Mary Lascelles remarked, 'He was not merely consistent, he was all of a piece throughout.'

After his father's death in 1933, he became his own land agent and for many years ran the estate single-handed, carefully balancing the needs of the house against those of his tenants. He restrained the urge to clean important pictures when he knew that the money was more urgently needed for the improvement of cottages, and found it necessary in 1934 to sell the best of William Windham II's splendid Van de Veldes to the National Maritime Museum.

'Wyndham, as he was only too ready to admit, was a shy man, and this was reflected in his conversation by the fact that he seldom ever looked anyone straight in the face; the glance from his large brown eyes always seemed to be sliding away from one. But there was nothing shy about his delivery, which flowed as smoothly as the Danube… It was certainly a voice that gave one the impression of having been nurtured on vintage port rather then on dry martinis.'

Brinsley Ford

In the hall and its gardens architectural repairs were the most pressing priority. In 1937 he restored the Dove-house and in 1958 he tackled the Orangery, which had been derelict since 1900. His architect was Donovan Purcell, who designed the simple mahogany lamp standards which were introduced into most of the rooms when electricity reached the hall in 1954 – long after the estate workers' cottages had been supplied.

The Felbrigg landscape meant as much to him as the house, and he loved trees. This is as evident from the extent and variety of his plantations as it is in the way that he writes about the estate management of the early Windhams. It was in the setting of his woods that Sir Brinsley Ford gives us a picture of 'the Squire', as he was locally known, in 1963: '… his portly figure made even more shapeless by an old mackintosh, his grey hair strag-gling onto his collar beneath a green pork-pie hat, his slightly gouty step supported by a walking stick.'

Wyndham Ketton-Cremer did not marry, and the central tragedy of his life was the loss of his younger brother Dick in the German invasion of Crete in May 1941. He writes about it most movingly at the end of *The Story of a House* and the last two chapters are

characterised by sadness and a wistful uncer-tainty about the future. Others felt it too and the less sensitive would sometimes ask him what he was going to do with Felbrigg. The Squire would respond gravely that it was to be left to a cats' home. In fact he had already made an approach to the National Trust in 1941, and its Executive Committee had accepted the property on merit, subject to satisfactory financial arrangements. He had been involved in the work of the National Trust since the late 1940s, when he had helped Alec Penrose, the Honorary Regional Representative, with decisions about the decoration of the Orangery at Blickling, and he became a valued member of its Regional Committee. On his death in 1969 Felbrigg and all its wonderful contents, its woods, its parkland and its farms were formally offered to the Trust. The Squire's conscientious care of the building and estate had left no heavy burdens for its new owners, other than the obligation to follow his example.

(Right) An oval mirror in the Dining Room

Family Tree

Owners of Felbrigg are shown in CAPITALS

Asterisk denotes portrait in the house

JOHN WYNDHAM = Margaret Clifton
(d.1475)

Sir JOHN WYNDHAM = Margaret Howard
(d.1502)

Sir THOMAS WYNDHAM = Eleanor Scrope
(d.1522)

Sir EDMUND WYNDHAM = Susan Townsend   Sir John Wyndham = Elizabeth
(d.1569)   of Orchard Wyndham   Sydenham
                                       (d.1574)

ROGER WINDHAM = Mary   Judge Francis Windham* = Elizabeth   THOMAS WINDHAM   Jane   John Wyndham = Florence Wadham
(d.1599)   Heydon   (d.1592)   Bacon   (d.1599)   (d.1608)   (d.1572)

Sir John Wyndham = Joan Portman
(1558–1645)

John = Katherine   (1) Elizabeth = THOMAS = (2) Elizabeth   Sir Joseph = Mary Wilson*   Sir George = Frances
Wyndham   Hopton   Lytton   WINDHAM   Mede   Ashe, Bt*   (c.1632–1705)   Wyndham   Davy
(d.1642)   (d.1622)   (1585–1654)   m.c.1644   (1617/18–86)   of Cromer
            m.1620   (d.1663)

Wyndhams   JOHN = (1) Jane Godfrey (d.1652)   WILLIAM = Katherine*   Mary* = Horatio   Francis = Sarah
of Orchard   WINDHAM   (2) Jane Townshend (d.1656)   WINDHAM I*   (1652–   (1653–85)   1st Viscount   Wyndham   Dayrell
Wyndham   (1622–65)   (3) Dorothy Ogle (d.1664)   (1647–89)   1729)   m.1673   Townshend*   (1656–
and   (4) Lady Frances Annesley   m.1669   of Raynham   1730)
Petworth   (1630–87)

ASHE = Elizabeth   Col. William = Anne   Joseph = Martha   James   Thomas = Anne
WINDHAM*   Dobyns*   Windham*   Tyrrell   Windham   Ashe   Windham   Wyndham   Edwin
(1673–1749)   (1693–1736)   (1674–1730)   m.1705   (1683–1746)   m.1715   (1687–1724)   (1686–
m.1709   of Earsham   1752)

WILLIAM WINDHAM II* = (2) Sarah Hicks* (1) = Robert   Charles*   John = Mary   John Wyndham = Elizabeth
(1717–61)   (1710–92)   Lukin   (d.1747)   (1709–80)   (1717–89)   (1732–65)   Dalton
m.1750   m.1734

WILLIAM = Cecilia Forrest   Rev. George William Lukin = Catherine   Joseph*   George = Marianne
WINDHAM III*   (1750–1824)   later Dean of Wells   Doughty   (1739–1810)   Wyndham*   Bacon
(1750–1810)   m.1798   (1739–1812)   of Earsham   (1762–1810)

Vice-Admiral WILLIAM LUKIN* = Anne Thellusson*   Robert*   George*   John*
(1768–1833)   (1775–1849)
assumed name of WINDHAM 1824

WILLIAM = Lady   Cecilia = Henry   Major-Gen.   Maria = (1) George Thomas Wyndham*   Marianne = Rev. Cremer
HOWE   Sophia   Ann   Baring   Charles   Augusta   (1806–30) m.1826   Charlotte   Cremer
WINDHAM*   Hervey*   Windham*   Ashe   Windham   (2) William, Viscount Ennismore,   Wyndham   (1795–
(1802–54)   (1811–63)   (1803–74)   Windham*   (1805–71)   later 2nd Earl of Listowel   (1804–42)   1867)
        m.1835   (1810–70)   m.1826   (1801–56) m.1831   m.1829

WILLIAM FREDERICK WINDHAM* = Anne Agnes Rogers   JOHN KETTON* = Rachel Anne
(1840–66)   (alias Willoughby)   (1808–72)   Blake
                                  bought Felbrigg 1863   (d.1885)

Frederick Howe = Katherine   John   ROBERT WILLIAM   Marion   Gertrude   Rachel = Thomas Wyndham
Lindsey Bacon Windham   Eveleigh   KETTON   (d.1898)   (d.1895)   Anna*   Cremer
(1864–96)   Batt   (1854–1935)   (1841–1932)   (1834–94)

WYNDHAM CREMER CREMER* = Emily Bayly*
(1870–1933)   (1882–1952)
added name of KETTON 1924   m.1905

ROBERT WYNDHAM KETTON-CREMER* (1906–69)   Richard Thomas Wyndham Ketton-Cremer (1909–41)